The Evidence for Christianity

Ralph O. Muncaster

HARVEST HOUSE PUBLISHERS

EUGENE, OREGON

ONE-MINUTE ANSWERS—THE EVIDENCE FOR CHRISTIANITY
Copyright © 2005 by Ralph O. Muncaster
Published by Harvest House Publishers
Eugene, Oregon 97402
www.harvesthousepublishers.com

Library of Congress Cataloging-in-Publication Data
Muncaster, Ralph O.
   One-minute answers—the evidence for Christianity / Ralph O. Muncaster
      p. cm.
   Includes bibliographical references.
   ISBN 0-7369-1578-8 (pbk.)
   1. Apologetics—Miscellanea. I. Title.
   BT1103.M88 2005
   239—dc22   2004022265

Printed in the United States of America

05 06 07 08 09 10 11 12 13 / BP-MS / 10 9 8 7 6 5 4 3 2 1

CONTENTS

EVERYONE HAS QUESTIONS

Most Christians know that God's greatest commandment is to love him with all our heart, soul, mind, and strength. Secondly, we are to love our neighbor as ourselves (Mark 12:30-31).

So, we must love God not only emotionally (heart), spiritually (soul), and with our actions (strength), but also with our *mind*. This means using the gift God gave us—our brains—to learn about him and the evidence that provides assurance of his existence and nature.

Then, if we are to love others as ourselves, we must consider the priority of the gifts we might give others. The most important gift a Christian can give anyone is not food, not shelter, not financial assistance—not even outward love. Instead, it is the gift of Jesus Christ. He himself commissioned his followers to go out and make disciples of all people (Matthew 28:19).

Think about it. If we truly love family, friends, and others, how can we not introduce them to Jesus Christ?

One-Minute Answers, especially when used in combination with the S.H.A.R.E. program (see the next page) is designed to break the ice and help you discuss God, Jesus, and the Bible with other people in an easy, conversational way.

How to Use *One-Minute Answers*

First, familiarize yourself with this book. Think of questions you have that you've always wondered about. Look through the pages and see if you can find an answer. Then simply browse through the chapters and read any answers that catch your attention.

Then attempt to carry the book with you when you can. It has been designed to conveniently fit in a pocket, a purse, or a backpack. Look for chances to talk about God, Jesus, or the Bible. It's much easier and more natural than you might think.

For example, in a discussion of current events (terrorist activities, issues dealing with morality, you name it) you can easily say something like, "By the way, you wouldn't believe what I read the other day..." At this point, it's simple and natural to launch into citing a few fascinating facts about God, Jesus, or the Bible that can lead to a discussion. Any such discussion can lead to questions, and *One-Minute Answers* can provide introductory responses. (For more helpful suggestions, see "How to Talk About Jesus" on page 133.)

The S.H.A.R.E Program

The Examine the Evidence tools—see page 138—coordinate together to provide 1) education to build belief and faith, 2) ready answers to common questions, and 3) topic-oriented booklets ideal for evangelism. Here's how to S.H.A.R.E.:

Study the Word and the evidence in support of the gospel. Read the Word daily. The book *Examine the Evidence: Exploring the Case for Christianity* is a thorough self-teaching course designed to prepare you to answer questions.

Hear others. Develop the habit of listening to others. In this way, you can develop relationship in a short period of time. And by hearing what others have to say, you can learn what keeps them from learning more about God or from embracing him. Look for opportunities to encourage questions.

Answer questions. Use *One-Minute Answers—The Evidence for Christianity* to deal with issues on the spot. With this tool, there is no need to be frustrated or intimidated—you can be ready with quick answers.

Respond and research. Immediate answers often lead to deeper questions. Respond with a follow-up get-together. Research any incomplete answers or remaining roadblocks using the references provided in *One-Minute Answers.** Look for chances to share the gospel.

Evangelize. When the time is right, let the person you've been talking to know of the gift of salvation

---

* References from the Examine the Evidence tools are listed at the ends of the question-and-answer pairings. Many more useful resources are found in the section entitled "Further References, Sources, and Reading" on page 140.

through Jesus Christ. Sometimes you'll find that in-depth study of a particular issue is helpful. The 48-page Examine the Evidence booklets are designed to break down such specific barriers to Christ. At its end, each one tells the reader how to establish a personal relationship with God.

*Be prepared to give an answer
to everyone who asks you to give
the reason for the hope that you have.*
—1 PETER 3:15

One

GOD AND HIS ACTIONS

---

1. Is there evidence that God exists?

Many people proclaim we could never *prove* the existence of God. Some even use this as an excuse for not believing in God. However, God's existence can be in essence proven using the same standards of proof that we use every day. In particular, his existence can be proven by definition (similar to the definition proofs used in solving algebraic equations). When God is defined as the Creator of the universe, we are immediately faced with the mutually exclusive alternatives as to whether the universe came about through a random process or by special creation (by God). Now we are in a position to prove mathematically that random evolution is impossible, leaving the existence of God as the only option.

A second form of proof is probabilistic proof, using statistics. Engineers build bridges and design cars based on probability. Physicists predict eclipses and send people to the moon based on probabilistic equations. The incredible prophecy in the Bible indicates divine inspiration, which can be proven using probability to the same degree that many common laws of physics have been.

The final form of proof that we use is legal proof. This is used for "one-time" events such as a robbery (or a resurrection). This form of proof, though less reliable than the first two types, requires things like eyewitness testimony and circumstantial evidence—things that are available to analyze, for example, the resurrection of Jesus and his claim to be God in human flesh. See *A Skeptic's Search for God.*

2. How can I trust evidence for a God I can't see, touch, or feel?

We can't see, touch, or feel magnetism either, but we trust it every day of our lives. (It's responsible for the generation of electricity.) Likewise, we can't see, touch, or feel gravity—only its effects—yet we know it exists, and we depend on it every day as well (or we'd all be floating off into space). Likewise, we can readily see the evidence of God. Take creation, for instance—the creation of the heavens and the earth and life itself has made God's existence and qualities obvious since the beginning of time. The Bible says that people are therefore, "without excuse" (Romans 1:20).

3. Isn't it circular reasoning to use the Bible to prove God with statistical prophecy?

This is not the case when outside sources are used to prove the divine nature of the Bible's inspiration beyond doubt.

First, we know that Old Testament Scripture was written hundreds of years before Christ (we have manuscripts actually written centuries before the time of Jesus—see chapter six). The Bible contains more than 600 specific, historical prophecies—all precisely fulfilled and verified by a variety of historical records (see chapter eight). Some of these prophecies include exact descriptions of amazing events. They also foretell names of people in key roles and even predict the exact years and days of the occurrence of some of the most important Biblical events—hundreds of years in advance. History and archaeology *outside* the Bible confirm the divine prophecies and insights *in* the Bible.

Second, the Bible contains many scientific insights, recorded some 3000 years before science discovered these facts (see chapter nine). Only in the last few centuries have discoveries confirmed these insights into physics, medicine, and other fields.

4. Why doesn't God simply reveal himself in a "blaze of glory"?

First of all, God did reveal himself this way during the formational period of the Israelite nation, while the Old Testament was being written down. At that time, there was no evidence from Jesus, and no Bible such as we have today, to provide evidence. Such demonstrations, therefore, seemed more warranted.

However, today we have everything that is necessary to believe. As indicated in question 1, we can virtually prove the existence of God using common human standards of proof. Beyond that, God expects us to seek him to build belief, and ultimately to accept him based on faith (Hebrews 11:6).

5. Do any other holy books provide evidence of God's involvement?

The Bible tells us to test everything and "hold onto the good" (1 Thessalonians 5:21). Furthermore, it tells us to use 100-percent-perfect prophecy to know if something is from God (Isaiah 46:10; Deuteronomy 18). The Bible passes this test superbly, with hundreds of specific historical prophecies that have all been fulfilled with no errors. There is no other holy book with significant fulfilled historical prophecy.

The Book of Mormon and the Mormon book Doctrine and Covenants, for example, have failed prophecies (even though they were actually written centuries after the fact anyway). The writings of the Jehovah's Witnesses are filled with failed prophecies. And the Quran has virtually no historical prophecies (the one historical example, Sura 30:2-4, technically failed according to Muhammad's own definitions). Other holy books of Eastern religions

(Hinduism and Buddhism for example) essentially have no historical prophecy.*

6. Why did God create people?

Although we can't know all the reasons why God decided upon creation, the Bible tells us it's God's desire for people to love and worship him (2 Kings 17:38-39; Mark 12:30; Revelation 4) and to be in an eternal existence in direct relationship with him (Matthew 7:21-23). The reasons God gave us life on earth are reflected in his greatest commandments (See Mark 12:30-31):

1. to learn how to love him and worship him

2. to use the talents and blessings he has provided to help others learn to love and worship him

3. and ultimately, to *test* our love for him through the acceptance of Jesus Christ as Lord and Savior

Since God's purpose for us is an eternal relationship with him, he wants to be with "perfect" people that love him. Since God knows that no one is perfect, he provides a means of forgiveness (through the blood sacrifice of Jesus). Life on earth tests our love of him by how we recognize and accept this sacrifice. To prove our love, God gave us free will to make a *choice* (real love is chosen, not forced). In sum, by providing us life on earth and revealing

---

* Ralph O. Muncaster, *Examine the Evidence* (Eugene, OR: Harvest House Publishers, 2004), pp. 361-365.

his nature while giving us a choice to show we really love him, God provides a way to bring people into heaven who really want to love and worship him.

7. If God wants to be with us eternally, why doesn't he just come to earth and be with us here?

God did come to earth—as Jesus—to demonstrate his love for us and teach us exactly how to be with him forever. Eternity is a lot longer than life on earth. And the "new heaven and new earth" (Revelation 21) will be unimaginably nicer than this earth. God exists in a realm beyond time and space, though he can choose to enter it at any time (as he did in the person of Jesus and on other occasions). But God's purpose for *this* earth is not eternal. It's *very* temporary. His purpose is to provide an opportunity for all of us to know him, follow him, and prove our love for him.

8. Doesn't the Bible teach us that love, giving, and service to others are God's "test" to allow people to enter heaven?

No. Although God wants us to love, give, and serve others, the ultimate issue is *our love for God, demonstrated by our acceptance of his gift to us—Jesus Christ.* The entire Bible clarifies this issue by

1. showing humanity's separation from him through sin

2. defining the need for redeeming us from sin by a blood sacrifice (before Jesus, animal sacrifice was used)

3. recounting the provision of Christ (God in human form) as the ultimate and perfect blood sacrifice

4. revealing that only through our belief in and acceptance of Jesus as Lord and Savior can we enter heaven (John 3:36; 14:6)

Understanding this is very simple: God loved us so much that he sacrificed his one and only son in a horrible painful death—even for people that hated him (John 3:16; Romans 5:6-8). By rejecting his display of ultimate love for his Son (who was God in human form), we are blatantly rejecting—and *not* loving—God.

The idea that "good" people go to heaven and "bad" people to hell is a human idea. It is not what God says (Ephesians 2:4-8). It would be foolish and arrogant to think we know more than God. All people fall short of God's perfect holiness and need to be redeemed by grace through Jesus (Romans 3:23-24). So trying to earn our way to heaven by "being good"—something taught by most cults, and even believed by many Christians—is futile.

9. If love and goodness are not a test for heaven, why does the Bible talk so much about them?

If we truly love God, our love for others will grow (Ephesians 4:20-24). Consequently, our "goodness" will grow. Jesus also taught that our love for others reflects our love for him as well (John 15:12-14). Certainly God wants our love for him (and others) to flourish. The problem is when some people starting thinking that loving others means they automatically love God—the real God of the Bible. Many such people don't know the real God at all. The Bible tells us to *seek* him.

Frequently, religions that actually reject the one true God teach the importance of love and service. People following false gods are often very sincere in their affection for others, thinking they are serving a real "god." Yet in reality, they show no love for the God who made them because they are rejecting his essential gift of love to everyone—Jesus.

The Bible speaks of love for others so much because, once our love for the true God is realized through a relationship with Jesus Christ, the Holy Spirit will inspire increased love for others in us in response to the second greatest commandment. The Bible clarifies that we can recognize the degree of spiritual maturity (for example, a person's commitment to Jesus) through the "fruit" a person produces—including love for others (Matthew 7:16).

10. If believing in and accepting Jesus is all that is required for heaven, couldn't evil people like Adolf Hitler accept Jesus at the last minute before death?

Yes. The Bible doesn't differentiate between degrees of evil (sin) as it relates to forgiveness, and it indicates that everyone has hope regardless of what they have done. It says there is "no condemnation" for those who are in Christ Jesus (Romans 8:1). Note the strength of this wording—*no* condemnation—*none*. Instead of concerning ourselves about justice for evil people, we can instead be thankful for hope for ourselves and our loved ones.

11. What is the real nature of God?

God's primary attributes are

- perfect love (1 John 4:16)
- perfect holiness (Revelation 4:8)
- perfect justice (2 Thessalonians 1:6)

It is difficult for us to understand how God could maintain all three of these characteristics at once. For instance, when he destroyed Aaron's sons because they didn't exercise proper procedures in his perfectly holy tabernacle (Leviticus 10:1-2), was the punishment perfectly just? Was it perfectly loving? We must realize we are mere humans attempting to understand something that God can control in dimensions beyond time and space. God has eternity and heaven and hell to work with. We can't know exactly how it all fits together, but we can know his nature and trust him to correctly balance things.

12. How can God be perfectly just if he would permit someone like Adolf Hitler into heaven if he were to make a "last-minute" confession and accept Jesus?

Of course it would be an enormous assumption to think such an evil person would suddenly change before death—but suppose he did. Since, as we saw in question 11, God has eternity to work with things incomprehensible to us (heaven and hell), he can account for that which is beyond our comprehension. We tend to think only of the pain of victims and families on earth.

We might reason out such an issue this way: First, God would show his perfect love by offering forgiveness and grace to a totally undeserving person. Second, the magnitude of evil that someone like Hitler causes is relative to human perception. To God, evil is evil. To his perfect holiness, the evil in *any* human heart is unacceptable. Yet in his perfect love, he will forgive any and all evil through a person's acceptance of Jesus. And third, the Bible teaches us that there are rewards to be allotted based on what people have done while on earth (Matthew 16:27).

Presumably, a last-minute repentant Hitler-type would be at the bottom of the list.

Again, instead of worrying about the most evil people and what God would do with them, we should be thankful that God has offered the option of forgiveness to all of us regardless of the extent of our sin.

13. Does God get angry?

Yes. In spite of what we sometimes think, anger is not the opposite of love. It sometimes shows love. Several times God showed anger against Moses or the people of Israel (for example, Exodus 32:9-14). And Jesus showed anger as well (Mark 11:15-18, for instance). In every case, anger was directed against sin. Humans get angry for many reasons—most often for selfish ones. Such anger is sinful because instead of being *against* sin, it's anger *for* sin, so to speak. If you need to evaluate a feeling of anger relative to God's anger, ask yourself if the anger is against sin, or if you're angry because something didn't happen the way you or someone else wanted.

14. If God is loving and forgiving, why would he send "good" people to hell?

We must remember that human standards are not God's standards. In comparison to his perfect holiness, even our passing evil thoughts are significant sins. In order to have a perfect heaven, people must be redeemed and sanctified (made holy) through the blood of Jesus. The Bible teaches that everyone falls short of perfect goodness (Romans 3:23) and that God freely justifies us through his grace (Romans 3:24; Titus 3:7).

Consider also that many total atheists are "good" by human standards. But God tells us that no one is good enough to get to heaven on his or her own (see Ephesians 2:4-8). God's test is our love for him. And when we simply love him—as we do when accepting Christ—God forgives whatever sins we have committed.

On the other hand, rejecting God's love and refusing the necessary redemption so freely given by him demonstrates that a supposedly "good" person is not really good at all. It shows pride, arrogance, and contempt. It indicates that a person is not willing to even take the time to "seek" God (Hebrews 11:6), let alone be subject to the Creator of the entire universe. Even judged by human understanding, would it really be "perfectly just" for God to allow such a person—who is totally thumbing his or her nose at God—into the perfect place he has created?

15. Are any sins unforgivable?

Yes, but only *one* specific thing. The Bible calls it "blasphemy of the Holy Spirit" (Matthew 12:30-32).

It is the deliberate, continuous, and ultimate refusal to acknowledge God's power in Christ through the Holy Spirit. This happens in someone with an irreversibly hardened heart—someone who will never ask for forgiveness.

In other words, this is an intentional and deliberate ignoring of the prompting of the Holy Spirit—forever denying his work. Anyone who has been exposed to the truth will have the Holy Spirit encouraging him or her to believe and accept Jesus as Lord and Savior. Complete and ultimate rejection of this prompting is the one and only "unforgivable sin." *All* other sins, no matter how horrible, can be forgiven through Jesus.

Some Christians are quite frightened of the "unforgivable sin," wondering if they have committed it. In general, people who have such a fear have it because they already know Jesus and understand the consequences of being separated from him. In such a case, there is nothing to fear since their acceptance of Jesus demonstrates their receptivity to the Holy Spirit (rather than blasphemy).*

16. Is God loving or judging?

God is both loving and judging. The Bible tells us of his love throughout—he expressed his enormous love through forgiveness and provisions, even

---

* *Quest Study Bible,* NIV (Grand Rapids, MI: Zondervan Publishing Co., 2003), p. 1403.

after his people intentionally disobeyed him. Most importantly, God expressed infinite love by coming to earth in human form as Jesus Christ and dying the most painful death to fulfill the perfect sacrifice. Humans typically understand sacrifice as a means of redemption (for example, paying a penalty when you've done something wrong). Imagine how great the sacrifice must be for *all of* human sins for all time.

However, it would be against God's nature to ignore sin by not judging it. It would not be just, and we know God is just (see Exodus 23:1-9; Matthew 23:23, Luke 18:7; Romans 3:26). We also know God is ultimate love. So how do we reconcile a just (judging) God, requiring sacrifice, with an infinitely loving God? An infinitely loving God would sacrifice even himself in a horrible way to pay the judgment of sin upon others—*even for those who hate him.* That's what Jesus did.

17. Doesn't the Old Testament reveal a "judging" God who is different from the New Testament's apparently "loving" God?

God is consistent and unchangeable (Hebrews 6:17). But people tend to perceive the God of the Old Testament as more "judging" because the judgments of the Old Testament are openly demonstrated in time. Therefore they are very readily understood by (and are relevant to) humans. For example, many of God's judgments in the Old Testament involve the physical destruction of cities and people.

In the New Testament, God's judgment points more to the eternal judgment Jesus spoke of extensively. People tend not to be so affected by the idea of eternal judgment because it's beyond their experience. However, that shouldn't prevent us from understanding that eternal judgment is far more significant than the temporary physical judgment experienced by people in the Old Testament. A close comparison of judgment in both testaments finds them to be comparable and compatible.

Likewise, one finds great evidence of God's love in both the Old and New Testaments. Again, it's only a perception that there is more "love" in the New Testament because in it Jesus (and others) expressed teaching about love in words. In the Old Testament, God's great expressions of love came through many of his actions, from the delivery of the Israelites, to the provision of daily manna, to continual forgiveness time after time in spite of their disobedience. See *Examine the Evidence,* pages 491-494.

18. Does God punish people?

Yes. There are many examples in both the Old and New Testaments of God punishing people. The Old Testament deals with God's purpose of the teaching of his ways (according to the culture the Hebrews knew). Often his teaching required what we consider today to be radical and severe punishment. The Bible makes it very clear that a good father punishes his children to teach them (Proverbs 3:11-12). God's dealings in the Old Testament were to teach not only the people of Israel, but us today (via the Bible).

Throughout the Bible, God also gave people repeated opportunities to repent and achieve forgiveness. In fact, if you are reading this and have not yet accepted Jesus, no matter how great your past sin is, the fact that you are still alive exemplifies God's amazing fairness in giving you this additional chance to show you love him.

19. Does God say we can't have fun?

God invented fun! But God created "pure and holy fun"—great-tasting food, beautiful scenery, and inspiring music. Some people equate sin with fun, and so the misconception exists that God is against fun because God is against sin. Humans, tempted by Satan, deformed God's perfect plan. Rather than enjoy food as God intended, many started eating to excess (gluttony). Many, for further examples, began drinking to excess (drunkenness) and started having sex improperly (adultery). So humans have corrupted God's pure and perfect plan of fun.

Two

JESUS

---

1. Is there really evidence that Jesus actually existed?

There is far more evidence for the existence of Jesus than for that of virtually anyone in ancient history. It exists primarily in the form of written documents and in archaeology. There are no monuments or coins displaying Jesus for two reasons: 1) he was not a king or leader warranting such things; and 2) the making of likenesses of created things for the purpose of idolatry was strictly forbidden by Jewish law, and this prohibition was extended to the making of monuments for any reason.

Though Jesus had just a three-year period of ministry and was relatively unknown, his words and actions were nonetheless documented by many people and then copied by thousands of others in order to pass on—even though they faced death to do so.

Archaeology has also uncovered many sites important to Jesus' life that are believed to be authentic—including his birthplace, the sites of his crucifixion and resurrection, and others. See *Evidence for Jesus*.

2. Isn't evidence for Jesus contained only in the Bible, thus leading to circular reasoning?

No. There is substantial nonbiblical, even non-Christian evidence for Jesus. First, there is a large body of evidence from groups such as the Gnostics who wrote the Nag Hammadi documents (for example, the "Gospel" of Thomas), which extensively references Jesus in spite of inconsistent and heretical teaching. Second, there are numerous non-Christian writings about Jesus, including mentions in the Jewish Talmud; by Josephus, a Jewish historian; by Herodotus, Tacitus, Suetonius, Phlegon, and Pliny the Younger; by the satirist Lucian of Samosata; and by the Roman emperor Hadrian. Even Muhammad, while giving the sayings of the Quran in the years around AD 622, wrote about Jesus, his virgin birth, and his many miracles, along with other New Testament facts. See *Examine the Evidence,* part 2.

3. What religions acknowledge Jesus?

Use caution when the name of Jesus is used. Is it the Jesus whose existence and life are documented by the vast body of evidence? Or is it some other "form" of Jesus, created to fit the agenda of a religious group? Acknowledging Jesus means believing in and accepting the true physical Jesus, who died for our sins just as described by the Bible (which has stood the tests of documentary authenticity—see chapter six.)

The real Jesus is *the* Christ—the title of a person— not a "Christ consciousness." Major world religions that accept the physical existence of Jesus include Christianity, Judaism, and Islam. But only Christians acknowledge the role of Jesus as defined by the Bible—God incarnate, the ultimate sacrifice for our sin, and resurrected Lord.

Derivations of Christianity (called *cults*—which include Mormons, Jehovah's Witnesses, and Christian Scientists) distort the biblical message. Cults deny Jesus his deity and role. See *Examine the Evidence,* chapter 33.

4. How can the false "Jesus" of a cult be recognized?

The following questions will help:

- Was "Christ" the description of a human being— Jesus—or some sort of "consciousness" or thought? (Some cults deny Jesus not only his divinity, but also his humanity. They consider "Christ" just a state of mind.)

- Did Jesus physically die *for our sin?*

- Is Jesus *fully* God, and is he *one* with the Holy Spirit? (Some cults think of Jesus as separate from God and regard his crucifixion as an unimportant act, not recognizing his role as a perfect sacrifice as the Son of God.)

- Did Jesus physically rise from the dead? (Some deny Jesus' resurrection, which denies his deity.)

When considering a religion's claims about Jesus, look at the holy books claimed as its authority. Christians using acceptable Bible translations as their authority vastly outnumber the cult derivations. Some groups (for example, the Jehovah's Witnesses) have rewritten the Bible, changing critical words to fit their doctrine. Other cults try to tie the Bible into their own recent "holy books" to give their books authority (the Mormons and Christian Scientists, for instance). Test any proclaimed holy book using the prophecy test (see chapter eight). Only the Bible will prove authoritative. See *Examine the Evidence,* chapter 33.

5. Does it matter which "religion" I follow as long as it acknowledges Jesus?

"Religion" is simply a definition of a group of people assumed to have the same theological beliefs. Yet "religion" (or the religious group's structure) is not the important issue. What matters is your *personal relationship with Jesus.* If you follow a religion that worships the wrong God (for instance, one that does not accept Jesus as part of a triune God) or does not love God by accepting the blood sacrifice of his only Son, Jesus, you are either not recognizing the real God or are not loving the real God. (This book and the books in the Examine the Evidence series outline evidence for the one true God.) See *Examine the Evidence.*

6. **Can Jesus be just a good teacher or a prophet, but not God or the Son of God?**

It would be a contradiction to claim that Jesus is a good teacher or prophet, but not (the Son of) God. Why? A good teacher teaches the truth and does not lie. Jesus maintained that he and the Father were one (see John 10:30) and often emphasized his deity. If he actually was not God, he would be a deceitful, poor teacher.

Likewise, a prophet of God proclaims 100-percent-correct prophecy. Several times Jesus prophesied he would rise from the dead after three days and also that he would "sit on the right hand of the Father" (Matthew 26:64). Therefore, if Jesus did not in fact rise from the dead, verifying his deity, he would not be a prophet.

7. **Is there any evidence supporting Jesus' virgin birth?**

Naturally we can't *prove* a virgin birth that took place some 2000 years ago. Even so, careful thought and logic indicate it to be true. First, we know that the Gospel accounts were widely circulated during the time of the eyewitnesses to the events of Jesus' life (see chapter six). Hence, those eyewitnesses could have easily corrected any faulty information. The Bible tells us that Joseph intended to divorce (end his betrothal to) Mary when he found she was "with child," but after confirmation of the virgin birth by an angel, he decided to marry her (Matthew 1:19-21).

So first, we know the eyewitnesses accepted this story—at least to the extent of not challenging the words of the Bible. Yet there is another point to consider. Having legal (not illegitimate) parents was of vital importance within the Jewish law for many reasons, not the least of which was property rights. It would therefore make sense that any doubts of Mary's virginity be tested physically; something that could (and may) have been easily done. While this is a logical surmise, the Bible does not address it.

8. Why is a virgin birth even important?

The Bible teaches that Jesus was both fully divine and fully human. If there was no virgin birth (that is, no "overshadowing" of the Holy Spirit) Jesus would have been no more than human.

Those who have trouble with the physical possibility of a virgin birth should consider that it is no more miraculous than many of the actions of God. In this regard, perhaps most relevant is the amazing creation of life in the first place. See *Examine the Evidence,* part 1.

9. Why is the crucifixion of Jesus important?

We may never know exactly why the system of sacrifice, especially blood sacrifice, was set up by God. But the concept of sacrifice seems embedded in humans (revenge as sacrifice for mistakes; noble sacrifice for others; and so on). We do know that God commanded blood sacrifice for sin (Exodus 29:36). Much of the Old Testament touches on what God considers sin and what he considers redemption. The blood sacrifice of animals (which were to be as perfect as possible) was the model to teach us of the future crucifixion. And the crucifixion of Jesus is clearly revealed as the ultimate sacrifice for sin, which all people need. So in God's terms, a *perfect* sacrifice—himself in human form—is the *only* sacrifice good enough to redeem his creation.

10. What is the difference between Jesus' being *the* Christ and the idea of a "Christ-nature" spirit?

Cults sometimes twist the biblical definition of Jesus to a mysterious "spirit-only" Jesus. At first it may seem like an innocent difference of opinion between Christ being human (the word *Christ* is the title of a person—meaning "anointed one") and able to die for us, and a Christ-nature, or "Christ-spirit." However, it becomes a big issue because a "Christ-spirit" teaching denies Jesus' blood sacrifice and even (according to some cults) sin itself. It directly contradicts the essence of the Bible. And it denies Jesus the very essence of his role as the redeemer of mankind. In the first century, the idea of a "Christ-nature" was part of a condemned heresy termed Gnosticism. So swift and strong was the church's reaction against it, that even Jesus' beloved apostle John wrote a "test" in the Bible about it (see 1 John 4:1-3). Later, creeds were developed to differentiate this false teaching from biblical Christianity.

11. What are some of the cults that are unbiblical?

The largest cults that attempt to position themselves as "Christian" but have major doctrinal differences from the Bible's teaching are the Mormons (Latter-day Saints), the Jehovah's Witnesses, Christian Science, the Unification Church, Unitarian Universalism and Unity School of Christianity. None of these cults ascribe to Jesus his role as the God-in-human-flesh redeemer described in the Bible.

12. How do we know that Jesus is the only way to heaven?

First, it is important to accept that the Bible is the *only reliable authority* on issues that go beyond our five senses, such as life after death. This can be demonstrated through the perfect-prophecy test (see chapter eight). Second, accepting that, we can readily see that the Bible proclaims that Jesus is the "way and the truth and the life," that "no one comes to the Father except through [him]" (John 14:6).

This "narrow" definition for those who will be being admitted to heaven is stated elsewhere even more specifically: "Whoever believes in the Son [Jesus] has eternal life, but whoever rejects the Son will not see life, for God's wrath remains on him" (John 3:36). Things could not be clearer.

13. Why is Christianity so narrow? It doesn't seem fair!

God is God, and we are humans. It is not up to us to judge what is too narrow, or what is fair. However, it *is* up to us—and it's a very good idea—to determine what is true and act accordingly.

Instead of brooding over the question of fairness, it makes more sense to spend time being grateful that God provided a means of redemption. Furthermore, we should be grateful he made the decision to accept Jesus so simple—and that evidence for Jesus is so abundant. The bottom line is, the choice to accept Jesus is simple, straightforward, and free. It is available to anyone, regardless of their past.

14. What about people in jungles, aborted babies, and mentally incapable people who never have a chance to hear about Jesus? What happens to them?

The Bible indicates that everyone has an inherent knowledge of the existence of God, and through seeking him, a person can find Jesus, regardless of where he or she is. One example is how Peter was sent to Cornelius by an angel (Acts 10). Presumably, missionaries are sent likewise today.

However, it is best not to read into the Bible things that are not clearly stated. It would be a mistake to draw hard and fast conclusions about difficult issues that are not clearly explained. In reality, issues like those involving babies who die before birth and mentally incapable people are beyond our control. But they are in God's very capable hands. We do know that he is perfectly loving and perfectly just (in addition to being perfectly holy). Therefore, that he properly deals with difficult situations is all we need to know.

15. Why did Jesus have to die such a horrible death?

There is no greater way to show love for someone else than to give your life for them. God demonstrated his supreme love by causing his own Son to die in the most horrible and painful way ever devised by humans. Such a powerful display of love has caused millions of people to take Jesus seriously through the centuries.

16. Did Jesus have any brothers and sisters?

The Roman Catholic Church and others are sharply divided on the issue of whether or not Jesus had natural brothers and sisters. At issue is the "perpetual virginity" of Mary proclaimed by Catholics.

Protestants feel strongly that Jesus had brothers and sisters (actually, half brothers and half sisters). While there are several indications of this in the Bible, the clearest reference is in Matthew 12:46-47, which indicates that Jesus had natural brothers "waiting for him" and differentiates them from Jesus' disciples (verse 49).

17. Why did Jesus tell people not to proclaim his miracles or call him Messiah or king, until Palm Sunday?

Several times in his ministry Jesus requested that no one be told about his miracles, such as the healing of the leper (Matthew 8:1-4), or when he instructed his disciples not to tell others he was the Messiah (Matthew 16:20).

We should remember that many people were claiming to be the Messiah at the time, and also that the idea of what type of Messiah was expected was controversial—with many anticipating a military-type Messiah. When news of Jesus' miracles "leaked out," he immediately started to draw large crowds. This alone became problematic as Jesus still needed time to "get away" (Mark 6:31-32), or to quickly redirect his efforts from one group to another (Luke 4:42-43).

There was also the risk of too much attention being drawn to him prior to his "time" when he was to become the sacrifice for the sins of the world. This all changed on Palm Sunday, however, because this was the day forecast in prophecy (Daniel 9—see chapter eight). On that day, when the Pharisees rebuked Jesus' disciples for proclaiming him the Messiah, Jesus answered that if they were silenced, even "the stones would cry out" (Luke 19:39-40).

18. If Jesus is God, why did he then have to pray to God to accomplish his miraculous will?

Many times Jesus went to a secluded place to pray (see, for example, Mark 1:35-39). His purpose was to serve as an example, recorded for all eternity, demonstrating the kind of relationship human beings should have with God the Father.

When Jesus came to earth, many theologians believe he "emptied himself" of his pre-incarnate power to become fully human, through still fully divine. (Theologians call this *kenosis*—see Philippians 2:7.) In this way, Jesus could serve as the ultimate example in a way that human beings can relate to.

All of the power Jesus displayed through his human example came from his "connection" with God the Father—a connection available to anyone. (In other words, God is a miracle worker waiting for us to ask for miracles in faith.)

19. Why did Jesus weep?

Jesus wept over the loss of his friend Lazarus, the brother of Mary and Martha (John 11:35). This might be puzzling to some, since Jesus obviously knew he was about to raise Lazarus from the dead (11:23). But again, this demonstrates the full humanity of Jesus, and also illustrates to us that it is acceptable to mourn, even realizing the great reward in heaven that awaits believers.

20. Why did Jesus wait to travel to see Lazarus and his sisters?

When Jesus was told that Lazarus was sick and near death, he took his time and waited two more days before traveling to see him (John 11:6). When he arrived, the sisters were distraught and were critical of him for not rushing there to heal their brother (11:21).

The reason why Jesus waited, however, he clearly stated to his disciples before he even left on the trip. He told them that Lazarus's sickness would not end in death, but in "God's glory so that God's Son might be glorified through it" (11:4). In other words, Jesus already knew the future and purposely waited so that God's glory would be apparent through him.

21. What does it mean when the Bible says Jesus is our "high priest" (Hebrews 3)?

Theologians define three "offices" held by Christ:

- *prophet* (Deuteronomy 18:15; Luke 4:18-21; 13:33; Acts 3:22)
- *king* (Isaiah 9:6-7; Psalm 2:6; 45:6; 110:1-2; Luke 1:33; John 18:36-37; Hebrews 1:8; Revelation 19:16)
- *priest* (Psalm 110:4; Hebrews 3:1; 4:14-15; 5:5-6; 6:20; 7:26; 8:1)

The role of priest is very significant because in God's instruction to the Israelite nation, only the high priest could approach God in the most holy part of the tabernacle (later the temple), called the holy of holies, through a very thick curtain (and only once a year). When Jesus was crucified, this thick "veil" was torn, allowing anyone access directly to God through the blood of Jesus' sacrifice.

Therefore, by undertaking the role of the high priest, Jesus offered himself as the ultimate sacrifice for divine justice to reconcile the church with God (Romans 3:26; Hebrews 2:17; 9:14,28). Furthermore, he became the continual intercessor for all who come to God through him (John 17:6-24; Hebrews 7:25; 9:24).*

---

* Walter A. Elwell, ed., *Evangelical Dictionary of Theology* (Grand Rapids, MI: Baker Books, 1984), p. 793.

Three

THE HOLY SPIRIT AND THE TRINITY

1. Exactly who is the Holy Spirit?

The first indication in the Bible of the Spirit of God is in Genesis 1:2 at the creation of the world: "The Spirit of God was hovering over the waters." The Hebrew word used for spirit is *ruwach,* which literally means "breath." This clearly indicates that the Spirit is someone separate from God the Father and from Jesus. It also indicates the Spirit is a being, not a "force."

2. Is there any evidence that the Holy Spirit exists?

Perhaps the Holy Spirit is more difficult to "prove" than God (where we can use analytical and statistical evidence—see chapter one) or Jesus (where we can use legal evidence—see chapter two). Even so, everyone can relate evidence they instinctively know to the Holy Spirit.

For example, since the beginning of time, mankind has instinctively known that God exists (even though some chose to intellectually reject him). Likewise, people have an inherent knowledge of right and wrong. (This of course does not prevent people from choosing wrong.) Finally, the Holy

Spirit will (often subconsciously) "warn" and "convict" people regarding their relationship to Jesus (John 16:8-11).

3. Is the Trinity three different gods?

The Bible makes it clear that there is only *one* God. Examples include the account of one God (*elohiym*, in Hebrew) at the beginning of creation, one God mentioned in the Ten Commandments (Exodus 20:2-3), and one God mentioned by Jesus in the greatest commandment (Mark 12:30).

"Christian" cults like to twist this when they deny the deity of Jesus or deny the existence of the Holy Spirit—claiming that one God could not possibly be the same as three. Yet we know that these and other references are actually referring to a single triune God. For example, the existence of the three persons was confirmed by the exhortation by Jesus to make disciples of all men by baptizing them in the name of the Father, Son, and Holy Spirit (Matthew 28:19-20). See *What Is the Trinity?*

4. What are the "functions" of each person of the triune God, and how do they fit together?

God the Father represents the ultimate authority figure: perfect in holiness, and the receiver of worship in heaven. *Jesus* is the redeemer, the source of life for humans and the intercessor with the Father.

The Holy Spirit is the counselor, the comforter in hardship, and the agent of the Father's will.

Together they provide people everything they need: 1) an authority to worship, 2) a redeemer for forgiveness, and 3) a counselor to guide. See *Examine the Evidence*, chapter 30.

5. **Is the Trinity mentioned in the Old Testament?**

As indicated in question 9, all three persons of the Trinity were involved in creation. In addition, when God gave the first of the Ten Commandments (Exodus 20:2-3), the wording indicated the three-in-one nature of God: "I [singular] am the Lord your God [*elohiym*, plural], who brought you out of Egypt, out of the house of slavery. You shall have no other gods [*elohiym*, plural] before me [singular]."

Of course, there are numerous places where God the Father is mentioned in the Old Testament, and the Holy Spirit is also referred to (see Numbers 24:2-3). Scholars also point to veiled appearances of Jesus (called *Christophanies*). One example of this is of Melchizedek (Genesis 14:18), who at a minimum appears to be a "model" of Jesus, if not the pre-incarnate Jesus himself. Melchizedek was honored as the "priest of God Most High" (Hebrews 7:1-2), and Abram gave a tithe (tenth of everything) to him—just as the Israelites were later told to give to

God. He also offered Abram bread and wine, possibly a foreshadowing of the Last Supper.

6. Is the Trinity mentioned in the New Testament?

We find the Trinity present at the beginning of Jesus' ministry. When he came to be baptized, God the Father was also present as he spoke from heaven (Matthew 3:17). And the Holy Spirit is recorded to have descended "like a dove," lighting on Jesus (verse 16).

Moreover, we find reference to the Trinity at the end of Jesus' ministry, just prior to his ascension, when he instructed his disciples to make disciples of all men and baptize them in the name of the Father, Son, and Holy Spirit (Matthew 28:19-20). And there are other New Testament references to the three Persons of the Trinity right through the book of Revelation. In its final chapter we find the presence and involvement of God the Father, Jesus, and the Holy Spirit (Revelation 22:17).

7. How does the Holy Spirit work?

Jesus told us that the Holy Spirit would come to work in the hearts of believers as a counselor (John 15:26; 16:7). We know that the Spirit of God works in humans through both conscious and unconscious guidance (Romans 8:14). This guidance can involve guilt over sin, leading in dreams, inspiration about what to say in various situations (Mark 13:11), and other ways.

Finally, we know that the Holy Spirit testifies to believers about their sonship with God, and intercedes on their behalf (Romans 8:16,26)

8. **How can there be *three* Persons in *one* God?**

The three-in-one concept of the persons in the Godhead (three Persons in one Nature) has been extremely difficult for people to understand. This alone has caused many to seek other answers or reject the Godhead completely.

However, there are some ways to help us understand it. First of all we can consider a mathematical analogy. Many people's basis for rejecting the Trinity is their thinking that $1 + 1 + 1 = 3$. Of course, this is one accurate relationship of three distinct numbers of one. However, an equally correct relationship would be the product of the three; $1 \times 1 \times 1 = 1$. This more accurately describes the Godhead.

Another way to conceive of three totally distinct things forming one inseparable "thing" is the idea of love. For love to exist there must be 1) a "lover," 2) a "beloved," and 3) the spirit of love. Taking any one of these out of the mix would destroy the concept of love completely.

9. What is the role of the Trinity in creation?

In the creation account, we find that both the person of Jesus and the person of the Holy Spirit were present. Thus the Bible indicates that each person of the Trinity had a role in the creation of the world. Apart from God the Father, we find the Spirit of God hovering over the surface of the waters (Genesis 1:2), and also Jesus' presence at the creation of *everything* (John 1:2).

Further, Psalm 33:6 explains that God "breathed" (a reference to the Holy Spirit) all of creation into existence. Paul explains the importance of the role of Jesus in Creation when he says that Jesus, "the image of the invisible God," is the one all things were created "by" and "for" (Colossians 1:15-16). Paul also proclaims that there is but one Lord Jesus Christ "through whom all things came and through whom we live" (1 Corinthians 8:6).

10. What is the role of the Trinity in reuniting people with God?

The Trinity is an essential ingredient restoring the relationship of God with people because it fully takes into account our *humanity* (through Jesus), our *spirit* (through the Holy Spirit), and our need to rely upon and commune with an *authority* (through the Father).

In other words, human beings needed the humanity of Jesus for the perfect sacrifice of redemption (Matthew 16:15-17). We also need the Spirit for full communication with God (John 3:34, Romans 8:26). And finally, there is the need for the connection of the humanity through the Spirit to an authority figure, provided by God (Hebrews 10:5-7).

11. What is the role of the Trinity in developing virtues and holiness?

Once people come into a relationship with God, the rest of their life is a time of development of virtues and holiness. *Sanctification* is the word commonly used to describe this process.

All three persons of the Trinity play a role in sanctification. God the Father is the *standard* for holiness (1 Peter 1:15-16). Jesus, through his sacrifice, is the *source* for holiness (1 Corinthians 1:30). And the Holy Spirit, who gives guidance through communication with the believer, is the *daily provider* of holiness (Galatians 5:16).

12. Why is the Trinity necessary for eternal life with God?

This question is a bit like asking God why he is what he is—which is essentially an impossible thing for a finite mind to understand (since God is infinite).

Yet a broad overview of the Bible provides some understanding.

God the Father loves the people he created. Meeting his standard of perfect love and holiness is required for ultimate eternal presence with him in heaven.

But mankind fell into sin in the Garden of Eden. From this point on, a means of redeeming mankind with the Father was necessary. Blood sacrifice was introduced as the method to atone for sin.

God then provided the ultimate blood sacrifice— himself, in the form of Jesus Christ, the only thing "perfect enough." The second Person of the Trinity is essential to accept in order to gain God's grace of forgiveness.

However, in proceeding in life with Christ, turning away from sin is not easy. So a counselor was provided in the form of the Holy Spirit, who gives daily guidance.

13. Why do cults reject the Trinity?

Cults typically establish doctrine that fits human desires (as opposed to the teaching of the Bible). Frequently they hold to a belief that humans are in some way "gods" themselves. The doctrine of the Trinity contradicts any such invented notion.

For example, why would someone who believes they are part god think they need a savior? Some religions deny the existence of sin as taught in the Bible. Why would a savior be necessary from something that is not real? Many cults believe that people can "earn" their way to heaven by doing what the cult doctrine demands. Why would the Father's grace matter?

Bottom line, cults are interested in promoting their own attractive doctrines rather than what the Bible teaches, as with the Trinity.

14. **Which religions reject the Trinity?**

All non-Christian religions reject the Trinity. This includes the world religions of Hinduism, Buddhism, Shintoism, Taoism, Islam, Confucianism, and Judaism.

As far as the religions trying to pass themselves off as Christian (the "cults"), the list includes Mormons (Latter-day Saints), Jehovah's Witnesses (Watchtower), Christian Scientists and other mind-science cults, Unity School of Christianity, Scientology, and the many New Age cults.

15. **If I believe in God but not in the Trinity, will I go to heaven?**

People who don't believe in the Trinity reject the God of the Bible. And if you don't know God as he is, how can you love him? You are loving (worshiping) something else. If you reject the Trinity, then what is being rejected? Often it is Jesus Christ. The Bible makes it very clear that only those accepting Jesus will have eternal life (John 3:36; 14:6).

16. Suppose I believe in God and Jesus but simply don't believe in the Holy Spirit?

As in question 15, how can we truly love a God we don't know? Rejecting the Holy Spirit is rejecting the foundational teaching of the Bible that indicates the Spirit is essential from the beginning (Genesis 1:2) to the end (Revelation 22:17). (There are 533 occurrences of the word *spirit*—in all its meanings—in the Bible.)

Moreover, rejecting the Spirit means rejecting the relationship of the Spirit to Jesus' ministry from its beginning (Matthew 3:16) to its end (Jesus' exhortation of evangelism—Matthew 28:19). To repeat, rejecting the Holy Spirit is essentially rejecting God and Jesus too.

Four

THE RESURRECTION

1. Why is the resurrection of Jesus important?

The physical resurrection of Jesus is the foundation of the Christian faith (1 Corinthians 15:12-19). Why? Among other things, the resurrection is absolute evidence that Jesus is God and that his words are true.

The Bible teaches many important things related to the resurrection, among them that it is a demonstration of God's victory over sin. But perhaps the most important aspect of the resurrection is the absolute assurance it gives us that Jesus was exactly who he said he was—God incarnate. Jesus prophesied that he would be killed and then rise from the dead in three days, and his prophecy was fulfilled perfectly. By verifying his deity, Jesus also verified all of his other claims and teachings as well. See *Examine the Evidence*, part 4.

2. Was Jesus' resurrection physical, or was just his spirit resurrected?

Some people regard Jesus' resurrection as "spiritual," not physical. The Bible is very clear on this point (see Luke 24:36-49). The resurrected Jesus ate, drink, and was touched (John 20:24-29).

It may seem easier to accept the idea of Jesus being raised as just a spirit. Some cults use this concept and even go so far as to proclaim a "Christ consciousness" within people—implying humans are "part God." This dangerous and prideful thinking tends to glorify people, placing them on a plane comparable to Jesus. The Bible's message is quite different. Jesus was not "just" a spirit, and mankind cannot achieve similar spiritual glorification. *Humans need Jesus' physical sacrifice* and his physical resurrection to life.

3. How can we believe a miracle as incredible as the resurrection?

Believing that God could cause a resurrection is really no more difficult than believing that God created life in the first place, which is the miracle we can most directly confirm as an absolute fact (see chapter five).

Look at the world around us. It teems with incredible life that somehow, at some time, came from nothingness. (The Hebrew word *bara* used in Genesis implies creation from nothingness.) Scientists have confirmed now that time itself had a beginning. Such life had to come about somehow.

The only explanation is a supernatural God existing beyond time and space.

And logically, if God can create life from nothingness, he could certainly resurrect Jesus from the dead.

4. **How can we be certain Jesus was really dead in the first place?**

It is sometimes proposed that Jesus really never died and later simply regained his strength and escaped from the tomb.

This idea is preposterous when we think it through. First, Roman soldiers were professional executioners. They did this for a living. Tens of thousands were crucified over the centuries.

Execution by crucifixion was a slow, painful death. Contrary to popular thought, it didn't take place through loss of blood, but typically by suffocation. Victims would hang by their wrists to support the weight. However, while they were hanging, the diaphragm would be pulled up and not allow breathing. To take a breath, victims would push off of the nailed feet. The process of death was a long "up and down" period, until lack of strength precluded breathing. Hence there would be no doubt when a person stopped breathing and was dead.

Sometimes, as with the evening of Jesus' crucifixion, it was necessary to remove bodies from the cross before sunset because of the Jewish Sabbath. In such cases, the victims' legs would be broken to hasten death by removing their ability to breathe. In the case of Jesus, the soldiers noticed he was already dead (was not pushing himself up to breathe). To be certain of his death, however, they thrust a spear up into his chest cavity. The blood and water that escaped were indicative of heart failure.

In spite of the certainty that Jesus was dead, if we consider the other half of the question, we can be equally certain he couldn't escape from the tomb. Consider a weakened man trying to find a hand-hold and roll a two-ton stone away from the inside. (Even the women approaching the tomb were wondering how it could be rolled away.) There is no doubt that Jesus was dead.

5. Why were people so concerned about protecting the corpse of Jesus?

The Bible tells us that the religious leaders approached Pilate to make the tomb secure. Pilate responded by commanding that the tomb be made "as secure as you know how" (see Matthew 27:62-65).

The reason for this is mentioned when the religious leaders said that Jesus had prophesied that he would die and come back from the dead. They stated that the disciples might steal the body and that such a deception would be "worse than the first" (verse 64).

The religious leaders' authority had been undermined by Jesus, who had referred to them as a "brood of vipers" (Matthew 12:34; 23:33) and "whitewashed tombs" (23:27), among other things. Both the Bible and nonbiblical sources show that many people were starting to follow Jesus and move away from the religious teaching of the day. Hence, Jesus was an enormous threat to the leaders.

The Romans were concerned because their goal was maintaining the peace in the region. Since religion was a particular "hot button," they had every reason to want to cooperate and try to prevent potential conflict from a new sect that could create an explosive situation.

6. How did the Romans guard the tomb?

The guard posted at the tomb was not a solitary soldier, as depicted in some paintings. A Roman guard for such a political prisoner would have consisted of 16 soldiers who would sleep in shifts, so that at least four soldiers were awake.

Furthermore, the penalty for any soldier who fell asleep out of the assigned time or who deserted was the same as that of the prisoner he was in charge of—in this case, crucifixion. So there was enormous incentive for all the soldiers to remain awake and not desert. Any reasonable person would have to ask, what are the odds, under those circumstances, that *all* the guards would have fallen asleep? See *Evidence for Jesus,* chapter 2.

7. What other security precautions were taken at the tomb?

Besides the posting of a guard, the Bible tells us that a seal was placed over the stone that covered the tomb (Matthew 27:66). This seal was a cord stretched across the entrance and embedded in wax in which the governing body's seal was impressed. Anyone breaking the seal without the captain of the guard's approval would face crucifixion. While it would not be physically difficult to break the seal, it served as a psychological deterrent.

In addition to all this, the stone that covered the tomb is estimated to have weighed about two tons. Hence, it would have required much effort to remove. See *Evidence for Jesus,* chapter 2.

8. Why would the disciples want to steal the body?

Sometimes the simple fact is overlooked that the disciples would have had no motivation whatsoever to steal the body of Jesus. If Jesus had really died without a resurrection, then all he would have been was a dead messiah. None of his claims would have been verified. His prophecy—that he would rise from the dead in three days—would have been false.

Hence, when we see such a dramatic change in the disciples—including their bold preaching and evangelizing—recorded by secular history as well as in the Bible, it provides excellent evidence that something happened—something that convinced the disciples who knew Jesus best, that he was who he claimed to be. (See also question 14 in this chapter.)

9. Did the disciples have reasonable opportunity to steal the body?

It's easy to make a simple statement such as, "The disciples stole the body." However, thinking through the real situation makes one realize the unlikelihood of this event.

First, we should consider that the disciples were in a state of disarray and confusion. After all, their Lord had been crucified. This would create considerable mental "shock" and probably even discord among them.

Second, any plan to steal the body would have required enormous thought and careful planning. A ragtag band—ordinary people—would have had to overcome a professional Roman guard.

Third, by Jewish law, travel was very limited on the Sabbath, making any plan difficult to execute.

In summary, to think that a group of ordinary people in a state of shock could devise a near-miraculous plan to overcome a professional Roman guard—for no purpose (why retrieve the corpse of a dead Messiah?)—is preposterous.

10. What would have been the consequences for the theft of Jesus' body?

Archaeology has uncovered a first-century engraving above a tomb outside of Nazareth (near Jesus' hometown) that indicates the penalty for grave-robbing was execution.

11. How do we know that Jesus' tomb was empty?

If Jesus' tomb had not been empty, there would be no Christian church today. The foundation of Christianity is the resurrection of Jesus—predicated on an empty tomb. If a corpse of Jesus had been produced, it would have ended Christianity, and no church would have ever existed. Since the development of Christianity is an "unbroken-growth time line" since that original event (see chart on page 89), we can be certain that the tomb was empty. See *Evidence for Jesus,* chapter 1.

12. What was the reaction of the religious leaders to Jesus' "disappearance"?

The religious leaders would have certainly been especially concerned about the empty tomb. The

Bible indicates they paid off the guards to spread the word that they had been "sleeping" (Matthew 28:12-15); and furthermore, they would appease the "governor." Naturally the guards would have been frightened about this, given the seriousness of the consequences for falling asleep.

But the religious leaders had power far beyond merely "buying off the guards." They would also have substantial influence over Jewish congregations. One can only imagine the effort the religious leaders would have put into attempting to "find the body" of Jesus. Certainly they would have sought out sympathetic friends, family members, and any cooperative disciples—all in an attempt to obtain any leads about where Jesus was.

13. What would have been the reaction of the Romans to Jesus' "disappearance"?

Since the primary goal of the Romans was to maintain stability and peace in the region, like the religious leaders, they would have used whatever means were at their disposal to attempt to locate the body of Jesus and put an end to his movement forever. We can envision them employing the use of soldiers to search the countryside and buildings in the city and to ask questions of "theft suspects."

14. **What was the reaction of the disciples to the crucifixion and resurrection?**

The disciples were confused and despondent after the crucifixion, and for good reason—they didn't fully understand (or believe) the prophecy of the resurrection.

However, when they saw the risen Jesus they were understandably overjoyed (Luke 24:41; John 20:20), though his first appearance to the group was met with some doubt. He had to explain he was not a ghost, and he encouraged the disciples to touch him and proceeded to eat food, demonstrating his physical presence (Luke 24:36-43).

Upon believing in the resurrection, the disciples sprang into action—embarking on a course that changed their lives forever. All gave up their previous professions in order to spread the word about Jesus. Only 50 days after the resurrection, Peter addressed a crowd of people at Pentecost explaining the resurrection of Jesus. Three thousand were added that day (Acts 2:41), and their numbers grew daily thereafter (verse 47).

The evangelism of the apostles continued nonstop in Jerusalem, and they began to do many miracles in the name of Jesus. This upset the religious leaders, who were seeing their "worst fear" taking place—a new, rival religion that undermined their authority.

After Peter gave a speech to the governing body of religious leaders, the number of disciples grew to 5000 men (and presumably women and children as well—Acts 4:4).

Later, intense persecution started. This caused the apostles to take their evangelism outside of Jerusalem, which only increased the rapid spread of Christianity throughout the world.

15. What was the reaction of the people of Jerusalem to the resurrection?

We would expect confusion among the people of Jerusalem. After all, they had the established religious leaders telling them about a stolen body and the disciples teaching and doing miracles in the name of a supposed dead man. The preaching of Peter and others forced the citizens of Jerusalem to make a decision.

The Bible gives an indication of the impact on the men within the city. When women and children are factored in, we might estimate that as many as 15,000 residents of Jerusalem may have become believers within days of the resurrection. This would have represented about 15 percent of the population—an unheard-of change in religious orientation, especially in such a monotheistic culture, which would presumably have difficulty in accepting the concept that of Jesus was also God.

16. Does archaeology support the crucifixion and resurrection?

Archaeology cannot prove an event like the resurrection, but it can prove that people believed it at the time.

Several sites have been identified that indicate early Christians venerated Jesus and believed in the resurrection. Among these are the sites of the crucifixion, resurrection, annunciation, and birth, and the house of Peter, where Jesus performed miracles (Matthew 8:14-17).

Perhaps most important is the vast body of manuscript evidence in support of Jesus. This falls into two key categories: 1) Old Testament evidence (for example, the Dead Sea Scrolls) that confirms that the many prophecies about Jesus were written prior to his life on earth; 2) the vast number of ancient copies of the New Testament, which provides substantial documentary evidence that the events of Jesus' life are accurately written in the Bible. See *Evidence for Jesus,* chapters 11–13.

Five

CREATION VS. EVOLUTION

1. Exactly what does *evolution* mean?

The word *evolution* simply means "gradual or continual change." However, in the case of origin of
life—the most frequent application of the word—
it means the process of the random development
of the first living thing from non-living matter,
followed by the change of that simplest form of
life into some 1.7 million species in the world today (as well as many others that have become
extinct).

2. Is there scientific evidence supporting creation?

The scientific evidence refutes evolution. And since
there are only two alternatives—random, naturalistic
evolution or design by a creator—scientific evidence
that demonstrates the impossibility of evolution
must therefore support creation.

Biochemistry has recently discovered that evolution is impossible even at the molecular level—so
how could it exist at the species level? The electron
microscope (essentially available only since the later
decades of the twentieth century) has allowed us
to see the vast complexity of the human cell—far

more complex than the most modern factory. Space scientists (astrophysicists) have "proven" that general relativity is fact, which means time and space had a beginning—just like the Bible says. Since 1992, the Hubble telescope and several deep-space probes have provided evidence about the beginning of the universe, never seen before—again supporting the Bible. Combining this evidence from biochemistry and astrophysics, we can compute that there couldn't possibly have been enough time and matter to have randomly produced a single reproducing living cell—let alone a parade of complex changes resulting in many species.

This is just the tip of the iceberg. Microbiology is filled with other creation evidence. Old theories of "missing links" and the random, synthetic origin of the crucial DNA molecule now are ridiculous. See *Dismantling Evolution*.

3. If the idea of evolution doesn't make sense, how did it get started in the first place?

Long before space probes and electron microscopes, the great scientists had no doubt about creation (including Newton, Galileo, and others). Then came Darwin and "higher criticism" of the Bible (a movement in which intellectuals of the late 1800s decided they knew more about the Bible than the original authors and translators—an idea since proven wrong).

Many years before Darwin, scientists had been striving to find a plausible explanation for life without relying on a supernatural Creator (God). Yet severe problems existed in other evolution-type theories until Darwin established the concept of natural selection—a process that seemed it might allow evolution to "work."

Darwin discovered that, if traits that would help a species survive occurred in sufficient numbers, it would create a species variation (natural selection). The original species-type might even become extinct. There is nothing inaccurate (or unbiblical) with this idea—and it *does* occur *within* a species. It's called *micro*evolution.

The problem came when *micro*evolution was "stretched" into a theory that could change one species into a totally different DNA-driven form (for example, a fish to a frog). This, termed *macro*evolution, has never been observed. Furthermore, it can be shown to be statistically unreasonable.

Many scientists quickly jumped on the evolution bandwagon. People began to think science = knowledge, and the Bible = stories. But at that time, scientists had incomplete information. They thought human cells were "blobs" of protoplasm, that the universe was infinite, that fossils would eventually prove evolution through revealing vast quantities of "missing links." All these notions contradicted the Bible.

So a battle between Darwin's "science" and theology erupted. However, every one of these scientific ideas has been proven wrong, just as we saw in question 2 in this chapter. Science has even discovered that life came about suddenly in great bursts—just as the Bible indicates. See *Dismantling Evolution*.

4. **Now that we have the tools and the information that uncover the problems with evolution, why are so many scientists and schools still teaching it?**

Unfortunately, old ideas still abound in textbooks and in people's minds. Schools still reject the teaching of creation, and new evidence is slow to filter down. Many scientists are specialists and don't investigate the evidence of creation. Like the average person, most scientists were also taught evolution was "fact." So there is a presupposition that evolution is true. And scientists are very slow to criticize their colleagues who make their living out of perpetuating evolution.

In Darwin's day, we didn't even know that germs produced infections. Sterilization was unknown, which resulted in the deaths of millions of people. The Bible, however, already had such "medical" rules. The Bible was even the "medical text" finally used to conquer the dreaded Black Plague. One can hardly imagine ignoring sterilization today. Yet the doctors of Darwin's time did. We are quick to use discoveries (such as sterilization), abandoning outdated ideas that cause physical death—yet we are so slow to reject absurd ideas that can lead to eternal death. In fact, some scientists have stated they would rather continue to search for an impossible, natural answer than accept a supernatural God.

5. **Do all Christians believe the universe is only a few thousand years old, in contradiction to what much current scientific evidence seems to indicate?**

Not at all. Many very committed Christians, many of them highly educated, believe that the universe is billions of years old. Others do believe the universe is only a few thousand years old. These two viewpoints, called "young earth" and "old earth" are debated among Christians. See *Examine the Evidence*, chapters 3 and 4.

6. **What is the "young earth" position on creation?**

Young-earth advocates hold that the universe is perhaps as young as 6000 years and probably not more than about 10,000 years old. This group emphasizes a literal understanding of the Bible. They also consider the genealogies in Genesis to be dependable chronologies, and view the six days of creation as literal 24-hour days.

Much current scientific evidence seems to contradict this viewpoint. On the other hand, God could easily have created the heavens and the earth (and life) within a short, young-earth time frame. No scientific explanation is necessary. Faith in God's ability is all that is needed. See *Examine the Evidence*, chapters 3 and 4.

7. What is the "old earth" position of creation?

Old-earth advocates accept the scientific record and believe the original language of the Bible to be flexible in regard to time specifications. They hold that current research findings of experts are compatible with the original, inspired language of the Bible by God, which allows more latitude than is often thought. (For instance, leading biblical scholars such as Gleason Archer and Walter Kaiser have supported the old-earth position as being entirely acceptable from a biblical interpretation standpoint.) See *Examine the Evidence*, chapter 3.

8. Why wouldn't billions of years allow for evolution?

Recent advances in molecular biochemistry have enabled us to understand the enormous intricacy of the living cell. Even the most simple cell conceivable would require a minimum of about 100,000 DNA *base pairs* (the nucleotide "rungs" of the DNA ladder), and a minimum of about 10,000 amino acids to form the essential protein chain.

While other things would also be necessary for the first cell, just these requirements alone demonstrate the enormous improbability that even a single cell of life could form randomly. Every single base pair (in DNA) has to have the same molecular orientation ("left-hand" or "right hand"). Likewise, virtually all the amino acids must have the opposite orientation. All must be without error.

The odds of randomly obtaining just the correct orientations would be 1 chance in $2^{110,000}$, or 1 chance in $10^{33,113}$! If a trillion, trillion, trillion combinations were attempted every second for 15 billion years, the odds of achieving all the correct orientations would still only be one chance in a trillion, trillion, trillion, trillion...and the trillions would continue 2755 times! Put another way, it would be like winning more than 4700 state lotteries in a row with a single ticket purchased for each. Statisticians concur this is impossible.

Molecular orientation is only one small problem that must be overcome to mathematically account for a random origin of life. And there are other, non-mathematical problems—for example, how is "life" added to non-living matter?

Finally, all the above calculations regarding the impossibility of random origin only address the first, very simple cell. There would still be the problem of the development of more than 1.7 million highly complex species. See *Examine the Evidence,* chapters 5 and 6.

9. Does the "big bang" imply evolution?

Absolutely not. Ironically, when the big bang model was confirmed as virtual fact through experimental confirmation of Einstein's theory of general relativity, some scientists feared confirmation of creation, not evolution. The reason is that general relativity (and the big bang) indicates that there was a beginning of time, matter, and space. This supports the words of the Bible in Genesis 1, and in many other places as well. See *Examine the Evidence,* chapter 4.

10. Do fossils support evolution?

Absolutely not. First, it's important to understand the difference between soft science and hard science.

Soft science is the study of something based on observation without empirical supporting data. These sciences include paleontology and anthropology. Such sciences tend to use pictures and stories. They imagine things and use artwork to try to explain something never observed. Since they are based on one-time events that cannot be tested (like the origin of man), they are prone to fantasy. A person can easily draw pictures of a story of how a reptile became a bird. (Fairy tales work the same way—think of pictures of a frog becoming a prince.)

Hard sciences are those that use empirical evidence based on experimentation. They are precise and can be used to build bridges, calculate eclipses, and put men on the moon. Such sciences include physics and engineering.

Those contending that fossils support evolution are in the minority today. The reason is, there are so many gaps in the fossil record, and no evidence of transitional forms from one species to the next. Many have tried to "fill in the gaps" with artists' renderings. But like the frog-into-a-prince story, a picture can be drawn of anything.

This lack is an enormous problem. A true transitional life-form would be something with a nonfunctional "partial" something—like a partial feather. The fossil record, however, shows evidence only of fully functional components in the vast abundance of species.

Finally, though, the fossil record *does* show a tremendous and sudden surge of species types all at one very short period of time. This has been termed the Cambrian Explosion. This evidence supports the biblical account of creation. See *Examine the Evidence*, chapter 2.

11. **Don't common body parts among creatures demonstrate common ancestors?**

No. Rather, if this demonstrates anything, it shows that the parts had a common designer. Nonetheless, some say that because humans, bats, and dogs all have elbows, this shows they all had the same ancestor—supposedly validating evolution. This makes very little sense. It would be like saying a skateboard "begot" a bicycle, which ultimately "begot" a car—just because they all have wheels. What makes more sense is that they all have the same designer. In both examples, a good designer recognized that a specific mechanism (be it an elbow or a wheel) served a particular function particularly well. A good designer would then apply that good design to various species (or products) requiring that function.

12. **Don't useless body parts, or the stages of development of the fetus, show inheritances from evolutionary ancestors?**

No. For years, the early developmental stages of the human fetus were claimed "evidence" of evolution. They showed what appeared to be a tail, a "yolk sac," and gills. Some argued it revealed evolutionary ancestors. Scientists now understand that we'd have major problems without any one of these parts. The "tail" becomes the tailbone—essential for connecting major muscles that enable such things as excretion. The "yolk sac" is the initial source of blood cells. The "gill slits" become the inner ear. Even tonsils, which today seem like a nuisance, appear to have a purpose. Medical scientists believe the purpose of tonsils is to protect the digestive and respiratory system from infections. When the notion of "useless" body parts comes up, we should look for *real* explanations. See *Dismantling Evolution,* chapter 5.

13. **Haven't scientists created some building blocks of life in the laboratory as proof of evolution?**

Yes—a few building blocks of life have been produced—in a process exhibiting irreconcilable problems. No, they certainly do not prove evolution! First, the Miller–Urey experiments of the 1950s, which produced life-specific amino acids, were carried out under artificial laboratory conditions that were far from those on the early earth. Furthermore, they produced much more destructive "tar" than useful amino acids.

Secondly, the wrong conclusion has been drawn even from this highly limited success. Producing just amino acids is such an infinitesimal part of the necessary components and organization needed for complex life, that it would be like claiming that random production of a speck of black ink proves that the *Encyclopedia Britannica* randomly evolved. See *Dismantling Evolution,* chapter 5.

14. **Do mutations cause evolution?**

Yes and no. Mutations are almost always destructive. For instance, how often would a randomly typed letter cause an improvement to a manuscript? However, on occasion, a mutation can add to the survivability of an organism. If such a mutation is passed on to offspring (it must occur in the sex cells), and if it survives in the population in sufficient numbers, it has the potential of causing a change. However, this rarely occurs.

Even when it does occur, the change is still within the DNA of the species—so the effect is one of *micro*evolution, not *macro*evolution (see question 3). In other words, the change is *within* the species, not *between* species.

Some have speculated that mutations can happen that would significantly change a species' DNA itself, resulting in a new species. However, there is no evidence to support this. In fact, statistical calculations show that mutations would be ineffective in producing such variation.

Moreover, there is no indication whatsoever that mutations are capable of actually *adding information* to DNA. Such addition of information is necessary to "improvement" in a macroevolutionary sense. See *Examine the Evidence*, chapter 7.

15. What is *irreducible complexity*?

Irreducible complexity is the term given to the need for *complete* systems to appear in an organism in order for them to function at all. This observation directly contradicts the premise of evolution.

An analogy might be that of the simple mousetrap. It is made up of several components, among them the block of wood, the hammer, and the spring latch. Without any one of these the mousetrap is useless. Evolution would claim that all elements of the mousetrap developed separately, slowly. But that would make little sense since the trap would not work without all parts all at once.

Yet the mousetrap is incredibly simple relative to, for example, the human eye. The eye has millions of parts—from such basic assemblies as the lens, muscles, pupil, and optic nerve to millions of rods and cones. Without any of the basic components, the eye would not work at all. So the problem that evolution cannot answer is how the eye came about in infinitesimally small increments, when all parts were needed at once. Creation answers this question. Evolution does not. See *Examine the Evidence*, chapter 8.

16. **Doesn't the biblical creation account contradict the scientific account of the order of development of the universe and the planet?**

No. The popular belief is that the Bible and science are at odds in the Genesis account of origins. A careful analysis of Genesis shows that it agrees with science. Two things are necessary to understand: 1) Genesis is not a science textbook, and not all steps of origins are described. 2) We must recognize the "frame of reference" of "the Spirit of God" being at the surface of the waters (Genesis 1:2).

When these factors are taken into consideration, we find there are ten basic steps of creation listed in Genesis, which agree precisely with the order of those steps according to science. (See chapter nine, question 2 for more details.) The accuracy of this revelation is astonishing. Not only did no ancient culture know anything about creation, but randomly guessing the correct order of the steps would have the odds approximating the winning of a state lottery with a single-ticket purchase. See *Examine the Evidence,* chapter 4.

17. How do dinosaurs relate to the Bible?

Dinosaurs are apparently not described in the Bible. Their fossils may have originated the notion of their surviving into recorded history. The idea that the "behemoth" (Job 40:15-24) and the leviathan (Job 41) are dinosaurs is not accepted by most biblical scholars. And there are large problems with the theory that dinosaurs were present on Noah's ark. See *Dinosaurs and the Bible.*

Six

MANUSCRIPT EVIDENCE

1. **How do we know that our present Old Testament is an accurate representation of the original manuscripts?**

An often overlooked fact in the development and transmission of the Old Testament is the importance it played in Israelite culture and government. The Torah (the first five books of the Old Testament) and later the entire Tanakh (that is, the Old Testament) were both the religious law and the administrative law of the land. Because the books were considered to be holy, they were held in the highest esteem, and the greatest care was given to the accurate copying of manuscripts from the original copies.

The process involved highly trained scribes. These men had many disciplines to ensure perfect copying. Apart from special preparation of paper and inks, there were many "tests" they employed to preclude mistakes. For example, the numbers of words and letters were added up and compared to the master scroll; the center letter in a scroll was compared to the center on the master. Scribes, although experts at Scripture memorization, were not permitted to write lines of verse from memory, but instead had to visually confirm each individual letter.

Ceremonially, a special prayer was said prior to writing the name of God, and master scrolls were even given a ceremonial burial when they had finally worn out. See *Examine the Evidence,* part 2.

2. How do we know the New Testament is an accurate representation of the original manuscripts?

There are far more ancient copies of New Testament scrolls than of any other ancient work. In fact, well over 5000 ancient New Testament copies are available for analysis today, versus only a handful of copies of other books that we take for granted as history. (One such example is *The Gallic Wars* by Julius Caesar, of which we only have ten ancient copies.)

Secondly, the New Testament copies we have were written much closer to the date of the original than other ancient works. For example, the oldest extant New Testament fragment was written within 50 years of the original, compared to, for example, a thousand years (in the case of *The Gallic Wars*).

The combination of many more copies to compare for consistency and a shorter time between copies and originals leads to a greater assurance of documentary accuracy. According to authors Norman

Geisler and William Nix, the present-day New Testament is "99.5 percent pure."*

3. What evidence is there that the Bible wasn't changed by the church to "suit its purpose"?

The importance of holy Scripture in the Israelite culture made it virtually impossible to deliberately insert inaccuracies. All scrolls in the nation would have had to be changed simultaneously—along with countless memories (Scripture memorization was common)—just to make one single change.

In later centuries, stringent rules were applied to maintain accuracy. If at any point the church had attempted to alter Scripture, scholars would have unearthed these inaccuracies and exposed them as error. Certainly the entire Protestant Reformation revolved around the Bible—not its exact words, but rather the *interpretation* of those words. This demonstrates how much ongoing examination has historically been done on the Scripture.

The invention of the printing press changed the Scripture's medium from hand manuscripts to mass distribution, and in the process it moved control of copying out of the hands of the church into those of the people. This further solidified the exact words and also placed a "bigger microscope" on any changes that might be attempted.

---

* Norman L. Geisler and William E. Nix, *A General Introduction to the Bible* (Chicago: Moody Press, 1980), p. 361.

Finally, the discoveries of ancient manuscripts like the Codex Sinaiticus and the Codex Vaticanus (see question 13) provide a means of comparing today's copies with very old manuscripts. See *Examine the Evidence,* chapter 12.

4. How do we know the Bible truly was inspired by God?

The Bible tells us to "test everything" (1 Thessalonians 5:21). It also gives us a test that validates something as from God—the test of 100 percent perfect prophecy (Isaiah 46:10; Deuteronomy 18:18-22). As we also note in chapters one and eight, the Bible contains hundreds of testable historical prophecies—all demonstrated to be 100-percent correct. Furthermore, the prophecies in the Bible are not vague generalizations (like those of many of today's psychics). They are detailed and specific, providing names of people, places, dates, and events. No other holy book or person has demonstrated such ability.

5. How is the Bible unique in its authorship?

The Bible originates from ancient manuscripts written centuries apart. Imagine getting just two authors from the same city in a room together today to write a major book on controversial issues. It would be difficult for only two people from the same culture to agree on everything.

Yet the 66 different books of the Bible were written over a period from about 2000 BC to about AD 100 by 40 authors. These authors were from vastly different cultures, backgrounds, locations, and circumstances. Yet they are consistent in a wide variety of highly controversial issues. Since "truth" must be eternal to be valid, it must be applicable today as much as it was 4000 years ago. The Bible meets that test of truth. Millions read it every day, and it demonstrates life-changing power on a daily basis.

6. How is the Bible unique in its survival?

The Bible survived the greatest obstacles imaginable. First, it is unusual for any ancient book to survive in any great number—and many disappear entirely. Reasons for this are, of course, apathy regarding preservation combined with the fragile nature of the materials. But in addition to the elements of weather and poor preservation, the Bible faced the most intensive eradication attempts of any book—ever!

During the period of persecution in the early centuries AD, Bibles were destroyed in vast quantities. Replacing them was slow and laborious since they could only be hand-copied. In 303, there was even an edict promulgated that anyone found with a Bible would be executed.

The testimony of Christians further validates this life-changing book. People readily gave their lives to ensure it would be passed on for generations to come. Early Christian martyrs must have believed it was an accurate and important message. Further, it's reasonable to assume that God's Spirit prompted such devotion. See *Examine the Evidence,* part 2.

7. What is meant by the word *canon*?

Canon simply means "standardized." But in biblical understanding it has the special importance of indicating that Scripture is from God—"God-breathed" (2 Timothy 3:16).

Almost all of the Christian world today accepts the basic canon of the Bible. The books that were recognized as canonical were judged to be

- *authoritative:* divinely inspired
- *prophetic:* 100-percent accurate
- *authentic:* contained writings known to be valid
- *dynamic:* gave life-transforming guidance
- *acceptable:* consistent with God's nature and attributes.

See *Examine the Evidence,* part 2.

8. How was the Bible canonized?

Some people believe that a group of men met in a room and simply determined the canon of the Bible. Nothing could be further from the truth.

There were three basic canons—the Torah (first five books of the Bible), the Tanakh (the entire Old Testament, essentially the Bible used in Judaism today), and the entire Bible containing the New Testament.

In each case, the writings went through a process of "popular canonization" first—meaning that a vast body of people (including eyewitnesses to events) had to accept the writings as holy books. Only after lengthy popular acceptance was each biblical canon formally recognized. See *Examine the Evidence,* part 2.

9. When was the Bible canonized?

The Torah was popularly canonized more or less as the events happened (about 1450 BC). Since the Israelites were participating in a great number of spectacular miracles of God, including such things as the parting of the Red Sea, the daily provision of manna, and the glory of God in leading them day and night, belief in what Moses was writing was not particularly difficult. However the formal canonization of the Torah didn't occur until sometime after the first exile, which took place in the sixth century BC.

The Old Testament canon was essentially "closed" (determined) no later than 167 BC. Jesus referred frequently to these Scriptures as if they were a preordained collection of works from God. No room for variance was ever suggested. The Old Testament canon was then officially approved by the Jews in AD 70.

Noted leaders in the church had essentially recognized the canon of the entire Bible by AD 200. This became official in 397 at the Third Council of Carthage. See *Examine the Evidence,* part 2.

10. What is the Apocrypha?

The Apocrypha is a collection of books written during the period of history between the Old and New Testaments. They are accepted in varying degrees by the Roman Catholics and Greek Orthodox Churches. The word *apocrypha* means literally "hidden," or "obscure."

Many apocryphal books exist, far in excess even of those included in Roman Catholic Bibles, which contain, among others, Tobit, Judith, 1 and 2 Maccabees, Wisdom of Sirach, and Baruch.

The books of the Apocrypha were recognized as "edifying" but were not considered "God-breathed." They were a part of many early Bibles, however, and even contained in Protestant Bibles (even Martin Luther's Bible translation contained the Apocrypha). However, eventually Protestants dropped these books from Bibles for economic reasons and because they were not considered inspired by God. See *Examine the Evidence,* chapter 11.

11. Why is the Apocrypha in some Bibles and not others?

The Roman Catholic Church gave *deuterocanonical* (secondary) status to these books in 1546. Protestants disagree with that status and reject the Apocrypha for these reasons:

1. They were not part of the Old Testament of Jesus and the early church.

2. While Jesus knew of these books, he never quoted from any of them, even though he often quoted the books recognized as canonical in the Old Testament (the Law, the Prophets, and the Writings).

3. Ancient Jewish writers who used the Greek Bible, notably Philo and Josephus, were acquainted with the Apocrypha but never quoted it as Scripture.

4. Church Fathers who were familiar with the Hebrew canon clearly distinguish between Canonical and Apocryphal writings. The writings of Melito of Sardis, Cyril of Jerusalem, and Jerome show their recognition of the difference between inspired Scripture and the Apocrypha. There is substantial evidence that virtually no leaders of the early church considered these books "God-breathed."

5. The apocryphal books were never declared to be authoritative Scripture until the Council of Trent in AD 1546.

6. Many scholars consider the apocryphal books to represent a "lower level" of writing than the books

considered canonical. They contain numerous historical and geographical inaccuracies and do not "breathe" the prophetic spirit so evident in canonical writings.

See *Examine the Evidence*, chapter 11.

12. How do we know the "right" books of the Bible were selected?

The Bible gives us guidance in determining what should be considered the word of God: "All Scripture is given by inspiration of God, and is profitable for doctrine, for reproof, for correction, for instruction in righteousness" (2 Timothy 3:16 KJV). The Greek word for inspiration is *theopneustos*, which literally means "God-breathed." The writers of Scripture were under the divine influence of the Holy Spirit as he gave them the words to write down.

Also, we should remember that much of Scripture contains prophecy, and people could not on their own predict the events given in Scripture. (See question 4 in this chapter and chapter eight.) Some of the guidelines scholars use to determine whether a book should be considered as divinely inspired are:

- Do the writings contradict any other section of Scripture in theology or in accuracy (geographical or prophetic)?

- Did the church Fathers refer to these books as inspired?

- In the case of the Old Testament, did Jesus quote from the book?

13. What are the Codex Sinaiticus and the Codex Vaticanus?

The Codex Sinaiticus is one of the earliest nearly complete biblical manuscripts in existence (*codex* means a handwritten book). It was found in a monastery at the base of what is believed to be Mt. Sinai (where Moses received the Ten Commandments). Discovered in 1859, the manuscript was originally written in about AD 350. It contains nearly all of the New Testament and over half of the Old Testament (monks had been carelessly burning pages of the manuscript, not realizing its significance).

Like Codex Sinaiticus, Codex Vaticanus represents one of the earliest nearly complete Bibles. Written in about AD 325, it may be, some scholars believe, one of the 50 Bibles originally ordered by Emperor Constantine. While the ravages of time have damaged (or destroyed) portions of Genesis and the end of the Bible, the majority remains intact. See *Examine the Evidence,* chapter 12.

14. What is the basis for English Bible translations?

Jerome, an exceptional language scholar of his day, completed the translation of the Bible from original languages into Latin in AD 405. This version, the Vulgate, became the basis of some English

Bibles, most notably that of the fourteenth-century theologian John Wycliffe.

All credible modern-day Bibles are the result of biblical translation teams of scholars working from the original Hebrew and Greek. Many utilize all the resources available including the Dead Sea scrolls (Old Testament) and the Codex Sinaiticus and Codex Vaticanus. (Cults will sometimes create their own "translations"—for example, the *New World Bible* of the Jehovah's Witnesses—but they are suspect.) **See *Can You Trust the Bible?***

Seven

HISTORICAL EVIDENCE

1. What does the Christian church claim regarding the historicity of the Bible?

The Christian church claims that the Bible is completely reliable historically. It contends that all events in both the Old Testament and the New Testament are historically true and are consistent with the historical record. Furthermore, it claims that it can withstand testing using modern archaeology.

2. Why is it important to know that the Old Testament is historically accurate?

The Old Testament is the foundation for the New Testament. It sets the stage for the coming Messiah. Historical inaccuracies would cast doubt on the fundamental claims of the Old Testament—including the important prophecies of Jesus, which are a major part of verifying Jesus' claim to be God incarnate. If the Old Testament were shown to be inaccurate historically, it would also cause people to question the Old Testament teaching about the nature of God and his desired relationship with humankind.

3. Why is it important to know that the New Testament is historically accurate?

The historicity of the New Testament is crucial because it is the record of Jesus Christ. If the New Testament were not accurate, then none of the story of the crucifixion and the resurrection—the foundation of Christianity—could be trusted. Christianity would be meaningless.

4. How can we avoid the circular reasoning of using the Bible to support itself historically?

Circular reasoning would imply that the Bible and only the Bible is used to support its own content. Certainly there are portions of the Bible that support other sections of the Bible. But there is also adequate evidence from nonbiblical sources that confirm large portions of the Bible. This evidence comes from secular archaeology and non-Christian writings. See *Examine the Evidence,* part 2.

5. Assuming the events in the Bible were originally recorded accurately, how can we know that they were accurately transmitted down to us?

As the chart below shows, there was a continual line of written communication from the apostles through the early church Fathers to the present day—which confirms the accuracy of the written record. There is much evidence from outside resources that corroborates this communication continuum. See *Examine the Evidence,* part 2.

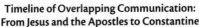

Timeline of Overlapping Communication: From Jesus and the Apostles to Constantine

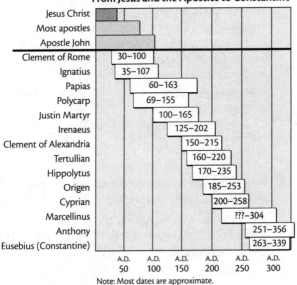

Jesus Christ					
Most apostles					
Apostle John					
Clement of Rome	30–100				
Ignatius	35–107				
Papias	60–163				
Polycarp	69–155				
Justin Martyr	100–165				
Irenaeus	125–202				
Clement of Alexandria	150–215				
Tertullian	160–220				
Hippolytus	170–235				
Origen	185–253				
Cyprian	200–258				
Marcellinus	???–304				
Anthony	251–356				
Eusebius (Constantine)	263–339				
	A.D. 50	A.D. 100	A.D. 150	A.D. 200	A.D. 250	A.D. 300

Note: Most dates are approximate.

6. What is "higher criticism" of the Bible?

In the latter part of the 1800s, fueled in part by Darwin's ideas on evolution, many began to distrust the Bible as being historically accurate. At that point in time, there was virtually no modern biblical archaeology to "test" this assertion.

7. **What is biblical archaeology?**

Biblical archaeology developed subsequent to
"higher criticism." Researchers, including such
great archaeologists as Sir William Ramsey and
William Albright, launched major expeditions to the
Holy Land and the Near East in attempts to disprove
(or find supporting evidence of) the Bible. The Bible
has consistently and emphatically met the test of
historical accuracy using archaeology. Evidence has
been so overwhelming that, in the case of Ramsey
(who once sought to disprove the Bible), he became
a Christian—calling Luke one of the greatest his-
torians of all time. See *Examine the Evidence,* chapters 15 and 16.

8. **Why do we not have direct archaeological evidence of the patriarchs yet?**

First, we must consider that the patriarchs were
nomads, and therefore did not build cities and
lasting monuments. Everything had to be portable.
So there were no written records of events.

Second, when the Ten Commandments were given,
idolatry was forbidden by God. This meant that
Jewish people would not have created monuments
and coinage to idolize any particular person or thing.

Other civilizations did not have these two limita-
tions. They were often stable, prideful empires that
would build monuments to their own glory.

9. **Is there *any* archaeological evidence of the period of the patriarchs?**

Archaeological evidence from the period of the patriarchs supports the cultural descriptions and events in the Bible. For example, there is evidence of Hebrew slaves in Egypt, and of the cities of Sodom and Gomorrah. There is also evidence of the existence of the early Hittites, of heavy doors as described in Lot's house (Genesis 19:9-10), of the early use of camels, and of the cities of Abraham (all questioned by higher criticism). There is even one archaeological site believed to be the grave of the patriarchs (Genesis 23; 25:9; 49:29-30). See *Examine the Evidence,* chapter 15.

10. **What evidence is there of King David?**

In 1993 a stone monument fragment was discovered at Tel Dan, near the border of Israel and Syria, that mentions King David and the "House of David," along with words implying a victory by the king of Damascus, Ben-Hadad, who "conquered Ijon, Dan, Abel Beth Maacah" (1 Kings 15:20). See *Examine the Evidence,* chapter 15.

11. **What evidence is there of the kings of Israel?**

There is substantial archaeological evidence of a number of the kings of Israel (from both the Southern and Northern Kingdoms). The type of evidence ranges from victory monuments (*steles* or *obelisks*) to fascinating finds such as a "receipt" to King Jehoiachin. (The receipt is a clay tablet that lists payment for rations of oil, barley, and other food to captives in Babylon, listing King Jehoiachin and his five sons as recipients—2 Kings 25:27-30.) See *Can Archaeology Prove the Old Testament?*

12. How can we trust the dating of events and people in ancient Israel?

Thanks to the Assyrians, archaeology can confirm the precise dates of the kings of Israel back to the time of Solomon. Excavations have uncovered lists of all kings of Assyria from 893 to 666 BC and the dates they took office (the *eponym lists*). The exact years for each can be established by using an eclipse in the capital city of Nineveh (May–June 763 BC— confirmed by astronomers) as a benchmark. The archaeological records of King Shalmaneser III (858–824) discuss the great battle of the last year of King Ahab of Israel's reign. Since the Bible specifies the succession of kings of Israel and the lengths of their reigns, it is easy to establish the dates of each. See *Examine the Evidence*, chapter 15.

13. How can we know that archaeological sites relating to Jesus are authentic?

The amount of support for authenticity varies by site. In many cases, the Roman government attempted to eradicate the venerated sites of Jesus by erecting pagan monuments (as in the cases of the sites of Jesus' birth, crucifixion, and resurrection). However, obviously something so significant as these sites would be remembered for many generations. And the pagan monuments, in effect, served to mark where the sites were.

In addition, early Christians built churches over many of the holy sites. The original churches at several key sites were built by Emperor Constantine's mother, Helena, in the early 300s soon after Christianity was permitted in the Roman Empire. Through the centuries, as Palestine was overrun by non-Christian cultures, the churches were torn down and rebuilt. Archaeology has uncovered the earliest Christian churches in many cases. See *Can Archaeology Prove the New Testament?*

14. Besides the sites of his birth, death, and resurrection, what other archaeological evidence is there regarding the life and ministry of Jesus?

Many of the cities that Jesus visited during his ministry have been discovered. Further, such sites as the tomb of Lazarus, the house of Peter (where Jesus spent much of his time), the synagogue in Capernaum, and the site of the trials of Jesus have been identified.

In addition, there have been finds that confirm things described in the Bible. For example, the remains of a first century victim of crucifixion reveal details of this method of execution, and a first-century fishing boat shows a design identical to that described in the Bible.

There are also important finds relating to specific people. A stone was found with an inscription describing Pontius Pilate as the "prefect" of Judea, verifying not only Pilate's existence but his governmental position. An ossuary (bone casket) was found and is believed to be that of Caiaphas, the high priest who presided over the trial of Jesus (Matthew 26:57).

Archaeology has also uncovered several ossuaries from shortly after the time of Jesus' resurrection that display graffiti of crosses and words like "Jesus, let him arise." See *Evidence for Jesus*, chapter 12.

Eight

PROPHETIC EVIDENCE

1. Why is prophecy important?

The Bible tells us to "test everything" (1 Thessalonians 5:21). It furthermore tells us that only God knows the "end from the beginning" (Isaiah 46:9-10). Therefore 100-percent-perfect prophecy is the ultimate test of something being from God (Deuteronomy 18).

2. What are the basic types of prophecy?

There are three basic forms of prophecy:

1. short-term prophecies that are made and fulfilled in the lifetime of the authors of the prophecies
2. long-term prophecies that are made in one generation and fulfilled in another
3. end-time prophecies that are to be fulfilled at the end of time, or that deal with heaven, hell, or something else unknowable in the spiritual realm (like angels or demons)

3. What are the strengths and weaknesses of short-term prophecies?

Short-term prophecies were important to the recording of Scripture because they defined who the true prophets were. Since anyone falsely prophesying was to be put to death (Deuteronomy 18:20-22), it was obvious that false prophets would not be tolerated. Short-term prophecy identified the reliability of a particular prophet. As an example, when King David sinned by committing adultery with Bathsheba, the prophet Nathan prophesied (among other things) that the son to be born would die (2 Samuel 12:14). First, there was a prophecy of a son, and second that the son would die. Either of these being wrong would literally end Nathan's life as a prophet.

4. Why are long-term prophecies important?

Long-term prophecies are important because there is no chance that the prophets making the predictions contrived the fulfillment. This makes them valuable for skeptics in future generations in evaluating the divine inspiration of the Bible.

5. How many prophecies are there in the Bible?

Reckoning the number of prophecies in the Bible depends on the precise breakdown that is used. This author counts 23 separate prophecies in Psalm 22 alone, and 25 in Isaiah 53 alone. Using this method of counting, the author's research uncovers 467 historical Old Testament prophecies and 201 historical New Testament prophecies, for a total of 668 historically verifiable prophecies. Likewise, there are 105

Old Testament end-time prophecies and 237 New Testament ones. See *A Skeptic's Search for God,* chapters 18 and 19; *Does the Bible Predict the Future?*

6. **How does the Bible compare to the Quran in regard to prophecy?**

Islam, being one of the few religions that claims to be based on historical fact, claims that the Quran is likewise historical. However, the Quran fails miserably in a prophecy test when placed beside the Bible. As mentioned above, there are some 668 historically verifiable prophecies in the Bible. There is only *one* in the Quran (Sura 30:2-4), and even that one is wrong. It claims that after defeat by a nearby land (Persia), the Roman Empire would return and be victorious within a "few" years. These two events happened in 615 and 628, respectively. But even according to Muhammad, the word "few" meant from 3 to 9 years, and would therefore fail the test. Yet even if it were true, the odds of such an event happening are not particularly staggering, and it would still represent only a single prophecy, compared to hundreds of prophecies in the Bible. See *Examine the Evidence,* chapter 23.

7. **How does the Bible compare to the Book of Mormon and Doctrine and Covenants (another Mormon holy book) in regard to prophecy?**

The Mormons (the Latter-day Saints) also claim

their holy books are history-based and divinely inspired. However, they fail the test of perfect prophecy. The Book of Mormon, written in the early 1800s, was supposedly translated from golden plates etched before Christ. It "prophesied" that Jesus would be born in Jerusalem (Alma 7:10). Of course Jesus was born in Bethlehem Ephrathah in Judea. Some Mormons may claim that Bethlehem is a suburb of Jerusalem. Yet even the Book of Mormon indicates it to be a separate city (1 Nephi 1:4). Furthermore, in the time of Jesus, it took more than an hour to travel the distance from Bethlehem to Jerusalem. That would hardly be considered a suburb. Another failed prophecy in the Book of Mormon is in 2 Nephi 10:7.

Likewise, the Mormon book of Doctrine and Covenants made several prophecies regarding a temple to be constructed in western Missouri within a generation of 1832. Regardless of what definition of generation is used, none would span a time period of more than 170 years—and the temple has yet to be built. See *Examine the Evidence,* chapter 23.

8. **How does the Bible compare to the holy literature of the Jehovah's Witnesses in regard to prophecy?**

The Watchtower (Jehovah's Witness) organization has a history of faulty prophecy. They started predicting the end of the world in 1914. Later, they changed the prediction to 1918; then to 1920; then 1925; then several times more to 1942, 1975, and 1980.

9. How does the Bible compare to the holy books of the Eastern religions in regard to prophecy?

The Eastern religions such as Hinduism, Buddhism, Taoism, and Shintoism are philosophy-based, not history-based, and therefore do not deal with historical prophecy. See *Examine the Evidence,* chapter 23.

10. What are some precise prophecies about the nation of Israel?

Perhaps the most spectacular prophecies about Israel have to do with the two exiles. The first, which was completed in 586 BC when Nebuchadnezzar exiled Israel to Babylon, was foretold in detail by eight different prophets, with some making these predictions hundreds of years in advance.

The second exile, when the Jews were dispersed throughout the world, is even more amazing in its prophetic implications. God had promised that the Jewish name would remain "great" (Genesis 12:2-3). The Jews were separated from their homeland for nearly 2000 years (AD 70 to 1948). Yet their identity as a people remained. Never in the history of the world has a group of people maintained its identity when separated from its homeland for more than a generation or two.

In addition, it was foretold that the exile would occur and that the Jews would be "regathered" (Isaiah 11:11-12; Ezekiel 37:21-22); and furthermore, that the land would be given to the Jews forever (Genesis 12:7). Incredibly, and against all odds, in 1948 the Jews returned to Israel and then preserved their territory against an attack by the Arab nations. The Jews won and have remained in the land ever since. See *A Skeptic's Search for God,* chapter 15.

11. What is an example of a precise, trustworthy prophecy about an Old Testament person?

While there are many Old Testament prophecies of people, one of the most interesting is the prophecy of the specific name of the ruler who would allow Israel to return from the first exile. Isaiah prophesied in about 700 BC that "Cyrus" would allow the return from exile to "rebuild Jerusalem and the Temple" (Isaiah 44:28–45:3). This is particularly impressive because the prophecy was made more than 100 years before Jerusalem and the Temple were even destroyed and about 160 years before the birth of Cyrus! See *A Skeptic's Search for God,* chapter 15.

12. What is an example of a precise, trustworthy prophecy of an Old Testament event?

Daniel made a spectacular series of prophecies in Daniel 8, involving about 400 years of history. He prophesied that the Medes and Persians would overcome the Babylonian Empire (which was in power at the time), and further that the Persians would be the more powerful of the two (Cyrus became the Persian king). He then predicted that Greece, then a relatively weak nation, would rapidly conquer the Medo–Persian empire—fulfilled by Alexander the Great in an amazing three-year conquest of the region. Then Daniel prophesied that Alexander would have a sudden end (he died suddenly at a young age) and that his empire would be divided into four different kingdoms, which is precisely as history records.

Finally, Daniel predicted symbolically the fall of Israel to the Seleucids and the evil events of the reign of Antiochus IV, who forbade Jewish worship and desecrated the altar in the Temple with the sacrifice of a pig. (This resulted in the Maccabbean revolt, commemorated by the holiday of Hanukkah.) Many other details are provided in this amazing prophecy. See *A Skeptic's Search for God,* chapter 15.

13. What are some prophecies precisely describing what Jesus would be?

What Jesus would do and what his role would be are sprinkled throughout the Old Testament in many books and many prophecies.

However, two of the sections most abundant in such predictions are as follows:

- *Isaiah 53*, which describes Jesus as the Savior and suffering servant who would be "pierced" for mankind's transgressions. Twenty-five distinct prophecies can be found in this chapter alone.

- *Psalm 22*—often referred to as the "crucifixion psalm"—contains 23 distinct prophecies about Jesus, pertaining primarily to his death on the cross.

See *A Skeptic's Search for God,* chapters 18 and 19.

14. What are some prophecies precisely describing when and where key events of Jesus' life would take place?

Interestingly, there are two prophecies of this type that both pertain to important "beginnings" for Jesus.

First, Genesis 49:10 states that the "scepter will not depart from Judah, nor the ruler's staff from between his feet, until he comes to whom it belongs and the obedience of the nations is his." To the Jews, the passing of the "scepter" represented the loss of the royal prerogative to exercise the death penalty. This verse indicated that the Messiah would come before that event occurred.

However, in AD 11, when Archelaus, son and successor of Herod the Great, was deposed, that prerogative of imposing the death penalty was taken away from the Jews, causing the religious leaders to go into mourning because they didn't believe the Messiah had yet come. They were not aware that Jesus, born earlier in Bethlehem, was the Messiah.

A second important prophecy, one of the most important in the Bible, was the prophecy of the beginning of the Passion Week, when, for the first time, Jesus entered Jerusalem and allowed himself to be called "king" (otherwise known as Palm Sunday). Daniel 9:24-27 contains this prophecy. Essentially it numbers the days from a decree by the Persian king Artaxerxes to restore and rebuild Jerusalem until the "anointed one" comes. It then describes him being violently cut off (crucifixion) and the subsequent destruction of the city and the Temple (which happened in AD 70). Analysis shows that this prophecy correctly predicted to the exact day the date of Palm Sunday.

In regard to prophecies about locations, the birth of the Messiah Jesus was given precisely as Bethlehem Ephrathah (Micah 5:2). Interestingly, there were two Bethlehems in Israel at the time, one being closer to Joseph and Mary's hometown of Nazareth. But holy Scripture specified which of these two small towns would be the birthplace of the Messiah. See *Evidence for Jesus,* chapter 15; *A Skeptic's Search for God,* chapter 19.

15. **What is the probability of all of the Old Testament prophecies coming true in Jesus by chance?**

Of course, determining a probability for something like prophecy is speculative at best. Even so, statisticians (and people like engineers) often use "order of magnitude" to determine if something is reasonable or impossible. Such an approach might be used in trying to determine the likelihood of all Old Testament prophecies about the Messiah relating to one specific man—in this case, Jesus. When the author made a fairly conservative "guesstimate" using only 30 of the 100-plus prophecies, he arrived at a probability of all coming true randomly in one man of 1 chance in 10^{110}. This is about the same odds as those of winning nearly 16 state lotteries in a row with a single ticket for each. It would be deemed impossible by statisticians. See *A Skeptic's Search for God*, chapter 20.

16. **How do we know that the Old Testament prophecies of Jesus were not written after the events they predict?**

The discovery of the Dead Sea scrolls in 1947 provides certain evidence that the prophecies were not written after the fact. Many of these scrolls, containing complete books and fragments representing all of the books of the Old Testament except

Esther, were written more than 200 years before Christ. They were buried in caves by the Essenes in about AD 70 and lay hidden until accidental discovery in 1947.

The importance of these scrolls cannot be overstated. All of the prophecies about Jesus are contained within them. Since they were written prior to Jesus' time, there is no possibility they could have been subsequently changed—contrived for some purpose to deceive people.

Additionally, the scrolls indicate virtually no change in the content of the Hebrew text from the time of their writing until today. This demonstrates that centuries of copying maintained a high standard of accuracy. See *Evidence for Jesus,* chapter 17.

17. What important prophecies did Jesus make?

As indicated, prophecy is a test of something being from God. Jesus' prophecies about his own crucifixion and resurrection are recorded 18 times in the four gospel accounts.

In addition, Jesus prophesied that

- one of his disciples would betray him (Matthew 26:21; Mark 14:17-21; Luke 22:21-22)

- his disciples would desert him (Matthew 26:30-31; Mark 14:26-27)

- Peter would disown him three times (Matthew 26:33-34; Mark 14:29-30; Luke 22:31-34)

- the disciples would meet him in Galilee after he had risen (Mark 14:28)

Because Jesus' prophecy is flawless, we can therefore trust Jesus' claims to be God (John 8:58; 10:30; 17:11).

Nine

SCIENTIFIC EVIDENCE

1. Is the Bible scientifically accurate?

It's important to recognize that the Bible is not a "science textbook." In other words, there are not an abundant number of scientific references. However, when the biblical text refers to something scientific, it is accurate, despite the fact that it was written thousands of years before scientific research discovered it. See *Examine the Evidence,* chapter 9.

2. How can we reconcile the account of creation in Genesis with science?

The account of creation in Genesis 1 is actually confirmed by the scientific record for all the events the Bible mentions. However, not all events are mentioned (for example, the creation of dinosaurs). It is also important to realize that the beginning of Genesis 1 states the initial conditions of the earth (formless and void), and the frame of reference for God (at the surface of the waters). Interestingly, both of these factors (initial conditions and frame of reference) are vital parts of the scientific method. With these things in mind, we can see that the ten steps of creation in Genesis are confirmed by science:

- *Step 1* (Genesis 1:1-2): A "beginning"—the creation of the heavens and the earth. Science now knows, because of the confirmation of general relativity, that indeed even time had a beginning. And the creation of heavenly bodies is the first of the steps listed.

- *Step 2* (verse 3): Availability of light at the surface of the waters. (Keep in mind the frame of reference— "at the surface of the deep.") Science indicates that early planets have dense, dark gases, and that the early-earth atmosphere eventually became translucent, with some frequencies of light penetrating the gases allowing for photosynthesis.

- *Step 3* (verse 6): Separation of waters from the earth and the clouds in the sky. Science indicates that with light heating the waters, evaporation took place, forming clouds of water above.

- *Step 4* (verses 9-10): Formation of continents. Science indicates that the next step in early earth was intense volcanic and seismic activity that created the continents.

- *Step 5* (verse 11): Early vegetation. Of the listed steps, early vegetation would be next, according to science.

- *Step 6* (verses 14-18): Appearance of sun and moon and stars at the surface of the earth (again, it's important to consider the frame of reference). Vegetation would "breathe" carbon dioxide from early earth and give off oxygen. This, along with other factors, caused the dense, dark gases present to become transparent, allowing for the sun, moon, and stars to become visible. (Note that the Bible even tells the reader the purpose for the visibility of these heavenly bodies—to "mark the seasons and days and years.")

- *Step 7* (verses 20-21): Creation of sea creatures and birds. Science confirms that of the creatures listed, the first to appear were early sea creatures and birds.

- *Step 8* (verse 24): Creation of land animals. Science agrees that the final creatures that appeared prior to man were land creatures.

- *Step 9* (verse 26): Creation of man. Science confirms that the appearance of human beings was next.

- *Step 10* (verse 2:2): God was finished with creation. Science agrees (first law of thermodynamics) that nothing more has been created.

Why did God mention only some of the plants and animals in the account of creation? Nobody knows for sure, but it is apparent that only ones that had a direct bearing on human beings were listed. See *Examine the Evidence,* chapter 4.

3. Are there any times when information contained in the Bible led to a general scientific discovery?

One person who trusted the Bible as a scientific resource was Matthew Fontaine Maury, the father of oceanography. Maury read the verse in the Bible that describes "pathways in the sea" (Isaiah 43:16).

Believing that the Bible could be taken literally, Maury searched the oceans of the world and discovered and mapped major currents that have been used ever since for shipping and travel by sea. See *Examine the Evidence,* chapter 9.

4. Are there any examples of information in the Bible leading to a medical discovery?

In the 1400s and 1500s Europe was decimated by the dreaded Black (bubonic) Plague. Eventually leaders turned to theologians, who then turned to the laws of Moses in the Bible. By implementing laws for quarantine (Leviticus 13), handling of the dead (Numbers 19), and proper waste disposal (Deuteronomy 23:12-14), the Black Plague was eventually brought under control. See *Examine the Evidence,* chapter 9.

5. What other medical insights are contained in the Bible?

If we consider the proven medical benefits of stress reduction from forgiveness, love, and surrendering control to God, there are many references to medical benefits in the Bible. But apart from that there are also some specific references to medically related things.

For example, God commanded circumcision on the eighth day after birth. While circumcision was to symbolize a covenant with him, why on the eighth day? Medical researchers know that newborns are particularly susceptible to hemorrhaging from the second day of birth to the fifth day since the body's blood clotting substance, prothrombin, is not present in sufficient quantities then. On the eighth day it skyrockets to 110 percent of normal, making it the safest day to circumcise an infant.

Additionally, studies in the mid 1900s showed that Jewish women had a significantly lower rate of cervical cancer than the norm. The smegma bacillus, which can easily be carried in the foreskin of uncircumcised males, has been identified as a major cause of this cancer.

Another example is sterilization, which was not understood until the late 1800s yet was essentially imposed by the many laws regarding "washing" in Leviticus 11–13. See *Examine the Evidence*, chapter 9; and *Science—Was the Bible Ahead of Its Time?*

6. **What sort of biology, chemistry, agriculture, and engineering insights were recorded in the Bible long before science discovered them?**

The Bible speaks of each creature being distinct "according to its 'kind'" (Genesis 1:21-31; 7:1-16). Ironically, while we now know that crossbreeding of non-interfertile species doesn't work, evolutionary theory implies otherwise.

In regard to agriculture, the Bible specifies in the laws of Moses that the Israelites were to give the land a "rest" every seventh year (Leviticus 25:4-6). Today scientists understand this principle of "fallow"— that allowing the land a period to rejuvenate itself with nutrients will result in better long-term production.

In regard to engineering, the Bible provides precise dimensions and design criteria for the building of Noah's ark (Genesis 6:15). Modern engineering has calculated that the design given in the Bible is the best-suited for a "barge-type" vessel designed to survive rough seas. See *Science—Was the Bible Ahead of Its Time?; Examine the Evidence*, chapter 9.

7. What insights into physics does the Bible contain?

Several important laws and principles of physics are indicated in the Bible—none of which were discovered by science until thousands of years later.

General relativity, first proposed by Einstein in 1915 and later confirmed by a myriad of scientists and experiments, was alluded to in the Bible. A key aspect of this theory (now essentially a "law" of physics) is that time, matter, and space had a beginning. The very first words of Genesis—"in the beginning"—relate to this important principle. However, the beginning of time is also mentioned elsewhere (1 Corinthians 2:7; Titus 1:2; 2 Timothy 1:9).

The first law of thermodynamics (conservation of energy) indicates that matter and energy can neither be created nor destroyed (just converted). The Bible has many references to God's *completion* (that is, no more creation—see Genesis 2:2-3; Psalm 148:6; Isaiah 40:26; Hebrews 4:3-4,10; 2 Peter 3:3-7). Joule and Mayer both independently discovered this in the same year—1842.

The second law of thermodynamics (entropy), which states that all things in a closed system move from a state of order to disorder without a purposeful input of energy, is also referred to indirectly in the Bible (Psalm 102:25-26; Isaiah 51:6; Matthew 24:35; Romans 8:20-22; Hebrews 12:27; and 1 John 2:17). This was not discovered until 1850 by Clausius. See *Examine the Evidence*, chapter 9.

8. **What insights into astronomy does the Bible contain?**

The Bible, for example, indicates that the "earth hangs in empty space" (Job 26:7). It also indicates that the universe is expanding (scientists call this miraculously orchestrated event—precisely fine-tuned for man—the "big bang"). References include Job 9:8; Psalm 104:2; Isaiah 40:22; 42:5; 44:24; 45:12; 48:13; 51:13; Jeremiah 10:12; 51:15; Zechariah 12:1.

The Bible indicates that the earth is a sphere (Isaiah 40:22), and also that the stars are "uncountable" (Jeremiah 33:22). Science once thought they were easily countable and even tried to "catalogue" them (Ptolemy, in about AD 100). Now, we know there are about a billion stars in each of a billion galaxies. At a counting rate of ten stars per second, it would take more than 100 trillion years to count them, which is clearly impossible. See *Examine the Evidence*, chapter 9.

9. Does the Bible contain any insights into geology?

The hydrologic cycle was not understood until Perrault and Mariotte identified it in the 1700s. However, the Bible refers to it twice (Job 36:27-28; Ecclesiastes 1:7) See *Science—Was the Bible Ahead of Its Time?*

10. How do scientific insights in the Bible reveal it is inspired by God?

When an overview is taken of the specific scientific insights (more than 30), as with prophecy, we can begin to statistically analyze the likelihood of all of these insights randomly being correct thousands of years before their discovery by science. Such an analysis leads to the conclusion that something supernatural (God) must have inspired the biblical writers. See *Science—Was the Bible Ahead of Its Time?*

Ten

WHY GOD ALLOWS SUFFERING

1. If God is loving, why would he allow pain and suffering in the world?

It is because God is loving that he wants and allows us to love each other and also to love him. However, love demands a choice. This means allowing the choice to love or to hate. Anything taking away the choice to hate would also take away the chance to love. However, by allowing humans the gift to choose to love, God allows them to also make sinful and sometimes violent and bad choices (hate). These choices result in suffering. Sometimes choices lead to suffering many generations down the road.

However, there are other forms of suffering that are not caused by choice—for example, consequences of natural disasters. We can't always see God's ultimate purpose, but we can be confident that it fits into an overall plan for the world. We know it is God's will that not anyone be lost (Matthew 18:14). Christians can take solace in the promise that "in all things God works for the good of those who love him, who have been called according to his purpose" (Romans 8:28). In pondering suffering, we should stay focused on God's long-term plan of eternal life and fellowship with him. The days of suffering on this earth are virtually nothing in light of eternity. See *Examine the Evidence*, chapter 29.

2. In what ways does God use pain to teach us and protect us?

Pain can be used for many good purposes. It can teach us and protect us and be used to discipline us, judge us, and forgive us. Too often we think only of the discomfort of pain. Instead, we should try to consider the value that might arise from a painful experience.

We've all heard the proverbial story of the child who, after constant warning from his mother, decided to touch the hot stove anyway. He of course got burned, but he never touched a hot stove again. Likewise, God allows pain in our lives, especially when it comes from consequences of not following his commands. Solomon, the wisest man of all time, indicated that sometimes it takes a painful experience to make us change our ways (Proverbs 20:30).

If we are cut, it hurts. If we are sick, we don't feel well. Pain, in these cases is a protection device. It warns us that we are injured or sick. Furthermore, pain causes us to avoid using an injured area, such as walking on a cut foot—allowing it to heal. Or in the case of sickness, it should cause us to slow down and rest, again protecting us by allowing healing to take place. And the threat of pain can protect us from the consequences of sin. For example, threat of contracting HIV might prevent us from adultery. Sometimes God allows short-term pain for longer-term good. This was the case with Joseph, who endured years of pain, yet saved his family and the entire region from a deadly famine (Genesis 41).

3. **In what ways does God use pain to discipline us, judge us, and forgive us?**

Those of us who are parents recognize that it sometimes takes discipline and "pain" to teach a child the consequences for bad behavior. The "pain" of being deprived of some privilege can correct bad behavior. Likewise, our heavenly Father uses pain to *discipline* us. David speaks of being "afflicted" (Psalm 119:67) and how the resulting pain caused him to pay attention to God's decrees. The Bible also tells us to let God train us, by enduring hardship as discipline, knowing that it demonstrates we are sons of God, "for what son is not disciplined by his father?" (Hebrews 12:7).

The Bible tells us that it is impossible to please God without faith (even though that faith is to be based on reasoned belief stemming from seeking God first—Hebrews 11:6). And God uses pain to *judge* our level of faith. Abraham endured the pain of thinking he was going to be required to sacrifice his son Isaac. Yet when God recognized Abraham's faith, he provided a substitute instead (Genesis 22:13). God led the Israelites through the wilderness for 40 years, testing them to find out how they would respond (Deuteronomy 8:2). The Bible indicates sometimes God is testing us in the furnace of affliction (Isaiah 48:10). And the Bible indicates that suffering leads to development of perseverance and ultimately, character and hope (Romans 5:4).

In regard to God's *forgiving* us, the ultimate pain was the pain suffered by Jesus. Of course, physically, Jesus was nailed to a cross to suffer the most humiliating and agonizing death ever conceived by man. But perhaps an even greater pain was the emotional and spiritual pain of assuming the sin of the world—even of people who hated him. Keep in mind, Jesus never even attempted to defend himself at his trial, realizing his role as a redeemer for human beings (Matthew 27:14). So through the ultimate sacrifice—the pain and suffering of his son offered unconditionally to everyone—God grants the opportunity for forgiveness to all humanity.

4. Why would God give us free choice?

God's ultimate goal is that human beings love him, worship him, and exist in fellowship with him in heaven forever. Therefore, if love of God is a goal, then the ability to love is necessary (Mark 12:30).

Nobody can force love. It must be a choice made by free will. So in order for God to allow humans the choice to love him, He had to provide free will, or choice, despite knowing that evil would exist and that humans would often make the wrong choices. See *Why Does God Allow Suffering?; Examine the Evidence,* chapter 29.

5. **How can suffering be used for a stronger relationship with God?**

   Many people of the Bible recognized suffering as a means to get to know God better. David, when in anguish, often called upon God (Psalm 118:5) and became known as the "man after God's own heart." Paul endured considerable suffering after leaving a relatively extravagant life as a Pharisee, yet spoke about suffering in terms of its ultimate benefits (Romans 5:4). And James, Jesus' brother, discussed how suffering can build character to be closer to God (James 1:2-8).

6. **How should we deal with suffering?**

   1. Talk to God about your suffering. He cares and will listen to you as you would to a child (Matthew 18:1-5; Luke 11:5-13; 1 Peter 5:5-7).

   2. Talk to others about your suffering. Choose a few close friends. Their listening will help you endure.

   3. Focus your thoughts on things that are true, noble, right, pure, lovely, and admirable. Do not be anxious

about anything, and pray about everything (Philippians 4:6,8).

4. Accept that although you may not understand the cause of your suffering, God will use it somehow for his purpose. In the previous questions we have addressed many ways God can use suffering for good. While enduring the pain, consider God's promises that suffering can be a tool for good (John 11:49-52); a tool for change (Proverbs 20:30); a tool for teaching (Hebrews 12:7); a tool to test your faith (James 1:6-9); a tool to improve you (Genesis 15:13-14); and a tool to build your character and faith (2 Corinthians 7:9; 1 Peter 4:19).

Eleven

BIBLE DIFFICULTIES AND APPARENT CONTRADICTIONS

1. Are there contradictions in the Bible?

There are places in the Bible that show apparent contradictions. However, if we take the time to research and understand the reasons for the perceived contradictions, they can become clear. One of the most common reasons for misunderstanding is not understanding the context of a particular passage. Another is misunderstanding the latitude and meaning of the original language (for example, rounding to a number of significant figures, as engineers would do in modern-day society). Also commonly, people jump to conclusions that there is a contradiction without thoroughly considering alternatives. See *Examine the Evidence*, chapters 31–32.

2. How do we reconcile the many differences in the Gospel accounts in the New Testament?

Much has been made among the differences of the four Gospel accounts of the New Testament. While this troubles some people, in reality it is a far stronger and more reliable overall testimony than if all four Gospels were identical.

Consider the testimony of eyewitnesses in a court of law today. Witnesses with accounts that are in agreement on the essential facts yet vary in details are considered far stronger than a group of identical witnesses. The reason is, it is human nature for different individuals to notice and stress different things. If all testimonies are identical, the account may be contrived.

Such is the case with the Gospel accounts of Jesus. In regard to the essential facts, they are alike. In details they differ, and even those differences can be readily understood with some thought. See *Examine the Evidence,* chapters 31-32.

3. How can we go about analyzing whether or not a contradiction exists?

Steps to analyze apparent contradictions are

1. *Overview:* state in simple terms the alleged contradiction

2. *Definition:* list all key elements that indicate a conflict

3. *Hypothesis:* state all potential means of resolving the conflict

4. *Research:* research necessary areas (possibly original languages, culture, and sentence structure)

5. *Judge:* decide if any alternative explanation is plausible, asking whether a resolution is truly impossible

When the above steps are employed, apparent contradictions in the Bible can be resolved. See *Examine the Evidence,* chapter 31.

4. **How can we explain the different order of creation in Genesis 1 and Genesis 2?**

A common mistake is to assume that Genesis 1 and Genesis 2 are two separate accounts of creation. They are not. They are two different "chapters" in a book. The purpose of Genesis 1 was to give the process of God's orderly account of Creation. This account is confirmed completely, in the order of steps, by the scientific record (see chapter nine, question 2).

Genesis 2, however, has an extremely different purpose. It discusses *what happened to heaven and earth once they were created,* with particular emphasis on creation of mankind, which is the focal point of God's work. See *Examine the Evidence,* chapter 31.

5. **Where did Cain get his wife?**

It's amazing how often this question is asked when the answer is quite apparent within the biblical text. Genesis 4:17 indicates that "Cain lay with his wife, and she became pregnant and gave birth to Enoch."

Yet up to that point in the Bible no females (except Eve) have been mentioned.

However, just because they hadn't been mentioned yet doesn't mean they didn't exist. It was common for cultures (and the Bible) to focus on the male line in genealogies. We read in Genesis 5:4 that Adam had "other sons and daughters"—one of which would have been a wife for Cain.

6. Isn't the Bible promoting incest with the early marriages?

At first marriage between close relatives was unavoidable as there were no other people available. One should consider, however, that the major physical drawback of close marriages is unfavorable (mutated) common genes that would have a higher statistical chance of being passed on. In the early days of mankind, the gene pool was not yet corrupted by the sin of many generations—those later generations leading to greater potential problems.

God is very specifically against incest, as stated in the Law of Moses (Leviticus 18:6-18).

7. Do the many names of God indicate an inconsistent God?

The Bible refers to God as *Elohiym* and *Yahweh,* and additionally as *Abba* ("daddy"), *Adonai,* and others. Critics wonder if this is truly one God.

First, we must recognize that the name of God is more than a mere label. It reflects God himself. Exodus 6:3 states, "I appeared to Abraham, to Isaac and to Jacob as God Almighty, but by my name the LORD *[Yahweh]* I did not make myself known to them." In essence, this indicates that God was appearing to the patriarchs as God Almighty *(el Shaddai)* but not yet the miraculous, covenant-keeping God about to deliver his people from bondage.

Second, consider the vastness of God. To attempt to fully recognize his many attributes, many names are required. See *Examine the Evidence,* chapter 31.

8. Is the Old Testament God a God of wrath, and the New Testament God a God of love?

Some people mistakenly think the God of the Old Testament is one of wrath, and the God of the New Testament is one of love—showing an inconsistent God. The basis behind this belief is that the examples of God's wrath in the Old Testament are often in terms humans relate to—death on earth. However, thorough studying of the New Testament reveals that God displays equal wrath (judgment) in the New Testament— the difference is that it's directed to eternal existence, which seems somewhat removed from human perception.

Likewise, there are many examples of love throughout the Old Testament, including such major things as the Israelites' release from the bondage in Egypt, daily provision of manna to them, assistance in conquering of the Promised Land, and repeated forgiveness in spite of disobedience. In summary, careful examination reveals a totally consistent God. See *Examine the Evidence,* chapter 31.

9. How can the different genealogies of Jesus be reconciled?

The genealogy of Jesus in Matthew 1 differs from the genealogy of Luke 3. How can these both be for Jesus? The genealogy in Matthew represents the line of Jesus through his legal father, Joseph (Matthew, a tax collector, might logically be more interested in Jesus' "legal" line). And the genealogy in Luke 3 represents the line through Mary, Jesus' physical mother (Luke, being a physician, might be more interested in Jesus' "human" line).

Perhaps the biggest clue to indicate this are the words in Luke 3:23 that say of Jesus, "He was the son, *so it was thought,* of Joseph." This revealing statement gives credit to the "legal" stepfather role of Joseph. See *Examine the Evidence,* chapter 31.

10. How can we reconcile differences in the sequence of events among the Gospel authors?

The first important thing to understand is that each Gospel was written from a different point of view and for a different purpose. A good example of different styles are the descriptions of Jesus' cursing of the fig tree. Matthew tends to write in a topical sense, placing stories in order of importance, as in a news article today—and he does not speak of the cursing of the tree until after the cleansing of the Temple, which he apparently considered more important.

Mark, on the other hand, tended to write in more of a strict chronology, and he spoke of the cursing of the tree prior to cleansing the Temple (Mark 11:12-16). Yet both authors indicate that Jesus went to the Temple immediately upon his arrival on Palm Sunday (Matthew 21:12; Mark 11:11).

We note a similar sequencing issue regarding the temptations of Jesus in the desert, which would seem to show a difference between Matthew's account (4:5-7) and Luke's (4:5-12). See *Examine the Evidence*, chapter 33.

11. **Was Jesus entering Jericho (Luke 18:35) or leaving Jericho (Matthew 20:29; Mark 10:46-47) when he met the blind man (men)?**

In this case, modern archaeology appears to have provided an answer to an apparent contradiction. It was discovered that at the time of Jesus, there were two Jerichos—an old city and a new one. Therefore it was quite possible that Jesus was leaving one city of Jericho and entering the other.

There is also an apparent difference on the number of blind men (one or two) in the different accounts. However, this can easily be explained by the importance of similarities and differences (see question 2). In one case the author is focusing on one blind man; in the other, on two. See *Examine the Evidence,* chapter 32.

12. Was Jesus' trial on Passover (Matthew, Mark, and Luke) or on the Day of Preparation (John 19:14)?

Most scholars hold to the traditional day of (Good) Friday as being the day of the crucifixion. Several things lead to this conclusion:

1. Many conclude that what we commonly regard as Palm Sunday was really "Palm Monday." (There is no scholarly reason for insisting that the day be Sunday, and other factors—such as a "missing day" in the Gospel accounts—suggest that Monday is at least as likely.)

2. They consider what John refers to as the "day of preparation" (for Passover) as coming into common parlance as Friday at the time. This is important because, in some Bibles, the Gospel of John (19:14) indicates the trial of Jesus was on the day of preparation, not on the Passover itself. It represents a translational difficulty. Was the meaning actually

that it was on a "Friday" or on the "day of preparation?"

The theme of Jesus modeling the ultimate Passover Lamb is carried throughout Scripture. In such a case, the perfect "Lamb" was selected on the tenth of Nisan (it would have been "Palm Sunday/ Monday") and would be sacrificed (crucified) on Passover—in this case Friday (or Thursday if the tenth fell on a Sunday).

In addition, by the time of Jesus, the Feast of Passover and the immediately following Feast of Unleavened Bread had been merged into one single feast coined "Passover Week." Hence, the "day of preparation" would be Passover—the initial day of preparation for a continuing weeklong event. See *Examine the Evidence,* chapter 32.

13. What was the actual hour of Jesus' crucifixion?

Matthew, Mark, and Luke indicate Jesus was crucified at the "third hour," darkness came on the "sixth hour," and Jesus "breathed his last" at the ninth hour (Matthew 27:45; Mark 15:25,33; Luke 23:44). John, on the other hand, indicates that Jesus was appearing before Pilate at "the sixth hour" (John 19:14).

This seeming insurmountable contradiction is simple to explain once we understand that John was using the Roman system of time (probably because of his longtime residence in the city of Ephesus, where the Gospel was written). It is universally accepted by scholars that the other three Gospels' numbering of time commenced at sunrise, as was the Jewish custom in Jesus' day. That would have placed Jesus' crucifixion at 9 AM—three hours after dawn.

The Roman system used by John is like ours; it has days that begin at midnight, and end immediately before midnight. (Elsewhere there are "hints" that John is using this system—see 12:1; 20:19.) With such a system, John would have Jesus before Pilate the sixth hour, and crucified about three hours later during the ninth hour—again, 9 AM. See *Examine the Evidence,* chapter 32.

HOW TO HAVE A PERSONAL RELATIONSHIP WITH GOD

1. Believe that God exists and that he came to earth in the human form of Jesus Christ (see John 3:16; Romans 10:9).

2. Accept God's free forgiveness of sins and gift of new life through the death and resurrection of Jesus Christ (see Ephesians 2:8-10; 1:7-8).

3. Switch to God's plan for your life (see 1 Peter 1:21-23; Ephesians 2:1-7).

4. Expressly make Jesus Christ the director of your life (see Matthew 7:21-27; 1 John 4:15).

Prayer for Eternal Life with God

"Dear God, I believe you sent your Son, Jesus, to die for my sins so I can be forgiven. I'm sorry for my sins, and I want to live the rest of my life the way you want me to. Please put your Spirit into my life to direct me. Amen."

Then What?

People who sincerely take these steps become members of God's family of believers. New freedom and strength are available through prayer and obedience to God's will. Your new relationship with God can be strengthened by

- finding a Bible-based church you like and attending regularly
- setting aside time each day to pray and read the Bible
- locating other Christians to spend time with on a regular basis

HOW TO TALK ABOUT JESUS

Understanding a Skeptic's Perspective

In order to share Jesus with a skeptic, it helps to understand where he or she is coming from.

Skeptics about Jesus (as I once was) generally think that Christians border on being fanatical. Often they feel that Christianity is used as a "crutch," and sometimes they even have some strange idea that embracing Jesus is like joining some sort of mysterious "cult." For these reasons, it is especially important to discuss Jesus in a gentle, matter-of-fact way, using language understandable to the secular world—not peppered with "Christianese."

However, nearly all skeptics have some degree of knowledge about Jesus and the enormous impact he has made on the history of the world, even on people's lives. This leads to many skeptics being either outwardly or inwardly curious about learning more about him. Additionally, the media has focused enormous attention on Jesus, in particular his historicity—as indicated by the regular appearance of articles in such magazines as *Time* and *Newsweek* and numerous prime-time television programs.

This media attention, especially in regard to Jesus' historicity, offers a particularly easy way to bring up the topic of Jesus in a non-threatening way. After all, if most people are being exposed to Jesus through the secular media, this makes discussing Jesus, especially beginning with the historical perspective, socially "acceptable" even to secular skeptics.

Preparing to Talk About God, Jesus, or the Bible

1. *Pray that the truth be revealed to the skeptic, and ask the Holy Spirit to guide you.* Prayer is powerful. Prayers about any discussion should center on asking for a skeptic's eyes to be opened (see 2 Kings 6:17). It's important to remember that God works through Christians and that Jesus promised his disciples that the Holy Spirit would provide them with the right words to say (Luke 12:12).

2. *Learn basic answers to the most common questions:* Why does God allow suffering? How can we believe in creation when "everybody" supports evolution? How do we know the Bible is inspired by God? Is the Bible historically accurate? How do we know the biblical manuscripts are trustworthy? Answers to these are provided in an abbreviated version in this book, and are covered in more depth in *Examine the Evidence: Exploring the Case for Christianity.*

3. *Develop trust and a sincere relationship with anyone you approach.* This does not necessarily mean a long-term effort to become close friends. A relationship

and a degree of trust can be built in about ten minutes, depending on the situation. This can be done at such places as Little League fields, airports, company picnics, and in many other situations. The key is to be sincerely interested in a skeptic's life, to be humble, and to be "yourself" (and especially not to be a self-righteous "Bible beater," which only builds walls).

4. *Try to understand the skeptic's world, and know when to back off.* Many skeptics fear a pushy Christian who will throw a lot of "Bible rules" at them in an apparent attempt to make them feel guilty and pressure them into Christianity. Remember that in the skeptic's mind, the Bible is not truly inspired by God and may be simply a collection of stories. It is better to start where the skeptic is—using undeniable history, examples of events in the secular world, or personal issues that lead into a discussion of biblical truth.

5. *Spend some time learning where to find evidence supporting the Bible.* This book is a good starting point for providing answers to questions that commonly come up. But *Examine the Evidence* and other helpful books listed at the end of this section and in "Further References, Sources, and Reading" provide far more depth on specific issues that arise. Many skeptics will demand such depth, and it is important to be confident that it exists and is available to you.

Starting a Discussion

Breaking the ice in a discussion of God, Jesus, or the Bible is usually the most difficult thing for someone new to spreading the good news about Jesus. My personal advice is, *think historically*.

Keep in mind that Christianity is a history-based religion. It is not philosophy-based like many others. For that reason, one can ease into a discussion by relating fascinating, undisputable facts to others that can open the door to discussion. Such facts are non-threatening and can be very interesting. Examples might include the following:

- Nebuchadnezzar, the hated king of Babylon who exiled the Jews in 586 BC, is actually a minor "author" of Scripture (Daniel 4:4-27)—which is considered inspired by God and is holy to both Jews and Christians.

- It was prophesied that the Jewish "name" would remain intact, and that the Jews would be return to Israel despite being dispersed (Genesis 12:2-3; 13:13-14; Isaiah 11:11-12; Ezekiel 37:21). Against all odds, this happened nearly 2000 years after the destruction of Jerusalem in AD 70.

- More than 100 prophecies precisely described Jesus—including the place of his birth, his role, details of his crucifixion and betrayal, and even the exact day he would enter Jerusalem as king ("Palm Sunday"). Mathematically, the odds against these prophecies coming about randomly are impossible. Only God's involvement can explain this.

There are many other examples, and often a discussion can be started based on some world event or some issue that has arisen in the skeptic's (or your) own life. Once a discussion is started, it's often amazing how easy and natural it is to continue discussing God, Jesus, and the Bible.

Sharing Your Testimony

Answering questions and providing evidence are extremely valuable—especially in this "information age." Nevertheless, the most powerful words for many skeptics are revealed in one's personal testimony (personal story).

Everyone should be prepared to give a brief, "one-minute testimony" at any time. Essentially, all it needs to contain is a description of your life before knowing Jesus and how your life has changed since knowing him. Be sure to share *how* to know Jesus.

Things to Keep in Mind

To sum up, discussions will be easier if you keep the following things in mind:

1. Look for opportunities—they often arise when least expected.

2. Build a degree of trust.

3. Listen first, talk second.

4. Avoid "Christianese." Use the parlance of the skeptic.

5. Ease into a conversation (for instance, use current events, personal experiences, or fascinating facts).

6. Look for opportunities to share the gospel.

7. Look for opportunities to share your own testimony.

8. Don't feel it is necessary to "convert" everyone at every meeting. Often moving someone closer to Jesus is all that is important.

9. Be sensitive about when to stop.

10. Make plans to follow up when possible.

Tools for Sharing God, Jesus, and the Bible
from Ralph Muncaster and Harvest House Publishers

Book-Length Resources

- *Examine the Evidence®: Exploring the Case for Christianity*

- *Evidence for Jesus: Discover the Facts that Prove the Truth of the Bible*

- *Dismantling Evolution: Building the Case for Intelligent Design*

- *A Skeptic's Search for God: Convincing Evidence for His Existence*

- *101 Reasons You Can Believe: Why the Christian Faith Makes Sense*

The Examine the Evidence® Booklet Series

- *Can Archaeology Prove the New Testament?*
- *Can Archaeology Prove the Old Testament?*
- *Can You Trust the Bible?*
- *Creation vs. Evolution: What Do the Latest Scientific Discoveries Reveal?*
- *Creation vs. Evolution VIDEO: What Do the Latest Scientific Discoveries Reveal?*
- *Dinosaurs and the Bible*
- *Does the Bible Predict the Future?*
- *How Do We Know Jesus Was God?*
- *How Is Jesus Different from Other Religious Leaders?*
- *How to Talk About Jesus with the Skeptics in Your Life*
- *Is the Bible Really a Message from God?*
- *Science—Was the Bible Ahead of Its Time?*
- *What Is the Proof for the Resurrection?*
- *What Is the Trinity?*
- *What Really Happens When You Die?*
- *Why Are Scientists Turning to God?*
- *Why Does God Allow Suffering?*

FURTHER REFERENCES, SOURCES, AND READING

General Reference

Archer, Gleason L. *Encyclopedia of Bible Difficulties.* Grand Rapids, MI: Zondervan Publishing House, 1982.

———. *A Survey of Old Testament Introduction,* rev. ed. Chicago: Moody Press, 1994.

Elwell, Walter A., ed. *Evangelical Dictionary of Theology.* Grand Rapids, MI: Baker Book House, 1984.

Geisler, Norman L. *Baker Encyclopedia of Christian Apologetics.* Grand Rapids, MI: Baker Books, 1999.

———. *A Popular Survey of the Old Testament.* Grand Rapids, MI: Baker Book House, 1977.

———. *Systematic Theology,* 2 vols. Minneapolis, MN: Bethany House, 2002 and 2003.

Geisler, Norman L., and Ron Brooks. *When Skeptics Ask: A Handbook on Christian Evidences.* Grand Rapids, MI: Baker Books, 1990.

Geisler, Norman L., and Thomas Howe. *When Critics Ask.* Grand Rapids, MI: Baker Books, 1992.

Geisler, Norman L., and William Nix. *A General Introduction to the Bible,* rev. ed. Chicago: Moody Press, 1986.

Glynn, Patrick. *God: The Evidence—The Reconciliation of Faith and Reason in the Postmodern World.* Rocklin, CA: Prima Publishing, 1999.

Hoehner, Harold W. *Chronological Aspects of the Life of Christ.* Grand Rapids, MI: The Zondervan Corporation, 1977.

Keller, Werner. *The Bible as History,* 2nd ed. New York: Barnes and Noble Books, 1995.

Payne, Barton. *Encyclopedia of Biblical Prophecy.* London, England: Hodder & Stoughton, 1973.

Smith, F. LaGard, commentator. *The Daily Bible.* Eugene, OR: Harvest House Publishers, 1984.

Stoner, Peter. *Science Speaks.* Wheaton, IL: Van Kampen, 1952.

Strobel, Lee. *The Case for Christ.* Grand Rapids, MI: Zondervan Publishing House, 1998.

Youngblood, Ronald F., Herbert Lockyer Sr., F.F. Bruce, and R.K. Harrison, eds. *Nelson's New Illustrated Bible Dictionary.* Nashville, TN: Thomas Nelson Publishers, 1995.

Zodhiates, Spiros, ed. *The Complete Word Study New Testament, King James Version.* Chattanooga, TN: AMG International, Inc., 1991.

Zodhiates, Spiros, and Warren Baker, eds. *The Complete Word Study Old Testament, King James Version.* Chattanooga, TN: AMG International, Inc., 1994.

Creation Versus Evolution and Analytical Evaluation

Alcamo, I. Edward. *Schaum's Outline of Microbiology.* Blacklick, OH: McGraw-Hill, 1998.

Behe, Michael J. *Darwin's Black Box: The Biochemical Challenge to Evolution.* New York: The Free Press, 1996.

Brouwer, Sigmund. *The Unrandom Universe.* Eugene, OR: Harvest House Publishers, 2002.

Darwin, Charles. *On the Origin of Species.* Cambridge, MA: Harvard University Press, 1964. This is the classic book introducing evolution. Obviously the author does not support its points of view.

Dembski, William A., ed. *Mere Creation.* Downers Grove, IL: InterVarsity Press, 1998.

Eastman, Mark, and Chuck Missler. *The Creator Beyond Time and Space.* Costa Mesa, CA: Word For Today, 1996.

Goodsell, David S. *The Machinery of Life.* New York: Springer-Verlag New York, Inc., 1982.

Grange, Robert. *A Scientist Looks at Creation* (videotape). Reel to Real & American Portrait Films. For information call 1-800-736-4567 or go to www.amport.com. The author highly recommends this videotape.

Heeren, Fred. *Show Me God: What the Message from Space Is Telling Us About God.* Wheeling, IL: Searchlight Publications, 1995.

Hoyle, Fred. *Mathematics of Evolution.* Memphis, TN: Acorn Enterprises LLC, 1999.

Milton, Richard. *Shattering the Myths of Darwinism.* Rochester, VT: Park Street Press, 1997.

Morris, Henry M., and Gary E. Parker. *What Is Creation Science?* El Cajon, CA: Master Books, 1987.

Muncaster, Ralph O. *Creation vs. Evolution* (videotape). Eugene, OR: Harvest House Publishers, 1999.

Ridley, Matt. *Genome: The Autobiography of a Species in 23 Chapters.* New York: HarperCollins Publishers Inc., 1999.

Ross, Hugh. *The Creator and the Cosmos: How the Greatest Scientific Discoveries of the Century Reveal God.* Colorado Springs, CO: NavPress Publishing Group, 1993.

————. *The Fingerprint of God.* Orange, CA: Promise Publishing Co., 1991.

————. *A Matter of Days.* Colorado Springs, CO: NavPress, 2004.

Schroeder, Gerald L. *The Science of God: The Convergence of Scientific and Biblical Wisdom.* New York: Broadway Books, 1997.

Spetner, Lee. *Not By Chance! Shattering the Modern Theory of Evolution.* Brooklyn, NY: Judaica Press, Inc., 1998.

Stewart, Don. *The Bible and Science: Are They In Conflict?* Spokane, WA: Aus-America Publishers, 1993.

Swenson, Richard A. *More Than Meets the Eye: Fascinating Glimpses of God's Power and Design.* Colorado Springs, CO: NavPress, 2000.

Wells, Jonathan. *Icons of Evolution: Science Or Myth? Why Much of What We Teach About Evolution is Wrong.* Washington, DC: Regnery Publishing, Inc., 2000.

Statistical Evidence

McDowell, Josh. *The New Evidence That Demands a Verdict.* Nashville, TN: Thomas Nelson Publishers, 1999.

————. *A Ready Defense.* San Bernardino, CA: Here's Life Publishers, Inc., 1990.

Walvoord, John F. *The Prophecy Knowledge Handbook.* Wheaton, IL: Victor Books, 1990.

Major Religions

Ali, Maulana Muhammad. *The Religion of Islam.* Columbus, OH: Ahmadiyya Anjuman Isha'at Islam, 1990.

Campbell, William. *The Qur'an and the Bible in the Light of History and Science.* Lake Forest, CA: L.M. Carter, n.d.

Cowell, E.B., ed. *Buddhist Mahayana Texts.* Mineola, NY: Dover Publications, Inc., 1989.

Dawood, N.J. *The Koran.* London, England: Penguin Group, 1993.

Gethin, Rupert. *The Foundations of Buddhism.* Oxford, England: Oxford University Press, 1998.

Goodall, Dominic, ed. *Hindu Scriptures*. Berkeley and Los Angeles, CA: J.M. Dent, Orion Publishing, 1996.

Halverson, Dean C., ed. *The Compact Guide to World Religions*. Minneapolis, MN: Bethany House Publishers, 1996.

McDowell, Josh, and Don Stewart. *Handbook of Today's Religions*. San Bernardino, CA: Here's Life Publishers, Inc., 1983.

Prabhupada A.C. Bhaktivedanta Swami. *Bhagavad-Gita As It Is*. Los Angeles: Bhaktivedanta Book Trust International, Inc., 1997.

References for the Old Testament

Free, Joseph P., and Howard F. Vos. *Archaeology and Bible History*. Grand Rapids, MI: Zondervan Publishing House, 1992.

Josephus, Flavius. *The Complete Works of Josephus*. Grand Rapids, MI: Kregel Publications, 1981.

Kertzer, Morris N. *What Is a Jew?*, rev. by Lawrence A. Hoffman. New York: Touchstone, 1996.

Shanks, Hershel, and Dan P. Cole, eds. *Archaeology and the Bible: The Best of BAR*. Vol. 1, *Early Israel*. Washington, DC: Biblical Archaeology Society, 1990.

References for the New Testament

Black, David Alan. *New Testament Textual Criticism: A Concise Guide*. Grand Rapids, MI: Baker Books, 1994.

Finegan, Jack. *The Archeology of the New Testament: The Life of Jesus and the Beginning of the Early Church*, rev. ed. Princeton, NJ: Princeton University Press, 1992.

Green, Michael. *Who Is This Jesus?* Nashville, TN: Thomas Nelson, Inc., 1992.

Habermas, Gary R., and Antony G.N. Flew. *Did Jesus Rise From the Dead? The Resurrection Debate*. San Francisco, CA: Harper & Row, 1987.

Habermas, Gary R., and Michael R. Licona. *The Case for the Resurrection of Jesus*. Grand Rapids, MI: Kregel Publications, 2004.

McBirnie, William Steuart. *The Search for the Twelve Apostles*. Wheaton, IL: Tyndale House Publishers, Inc., 1973.

McDowell, Josh, and Bill Wilson. *He Walked Among Us*. Nashville, TN: Thomas Nelson Publishers, 1993.

McRay, John. *Archaeology and the New Testament*. Grand Rapids, MI: Baker Book House, 1991.

Shanks, Hershel, and Dan P. Cole, eds. *Archaeology and the Bible: The Best of BAR.* Vol. 2, *Archaeology in the World of Herod, Jesus, and Paul.* Washington, DC: Biblical Archaeology Society, 1992.

White, James R. *The Forgotten Trinity.* Minneapolis, MN: Bethany House Publishers, 1998.

Evidence of the Bible's Accuracy

Blomberg, Craig. *The Historical Reliability of the Gospels.* Leicester, England: InterVarsity Press, 1987.

Bruce, F.F. *The Canon of Scripture.* Downers Grove, IL: InterVarsity Press, 1988.

Comfort, Philip Wesley, ed. *The Origin of the Bible.* Wheaton, IL: Tyndale House Publishers, Inc., 1992.

How We Got the Bible. Torrance, CA: Rose Publishing, 1998.

Price, Randall. *Secrets of the Dead Sea Scrolls.* Eugene, OR: Harvest House Publishers, 1996.

Vos, Howard F. *Nelson's Quick Reference: Introduction to Church History.* Nashville, TN: Thomas Nelson Publishers, Inc., 1994.

References for "Alternative Christian" Religions

Bodine, Jerry and Marian. *Witnessing to the Mormons.* Rancho Santa Margarita, CA: The Christian Research Institute, 1978.

The Book of Mormon. Salt Lake City, UT: The Church of Jesus Christ of Latter-day Saints, 1981.

Martin, Walter. *Cults Reference Bible.* Santa Ana, CA: Vision House Publishers, 1981.

———. *The Kingdom of the Cults.* Minneapolis, MN: Bethany House Publishers, 1996.

———. *The Maze of Mormonism.* Ventura, CA: Regal Books, 1978.

McDowell, Josh, and Don Stewart. *The Deceivers.* San Bernardino, CA: Here's Life Publishers, Inc., 1992.

Watson, William. *A Concise Dictionary of Cults & Religions.* Chicago: Moody Press, 1991.